Published by CFI Book Division
P.O. Box 159, Gordonsville, Tennessee 38563

ISBN-13: 979-8-9868765-4-2

Printed in the United States of America
Typeset in 11.5/13.8 Minion Pro

GOLD
TRIED
IN THE
FIRE

An exciting report of what
righteousness by faith has meant
to Adventists since 1888.

Robert J. Wieland

CFI Book Division
Gordonsville, Tennessee

Contents

Foreword

Faith is the magnificent New Testament treasure of motivating truth, which has not been adequately appreciated in many discussions of justification by faith. It means much more than what we call trust, for it has within it no self-centered basis. It is a heart appreciation of God's love [*agape*] revealed in the sacrifice of Christ. Such faith, being dynamic, enables the gospel to be truly the power of God unto salvation, for it works by love in both justification and sanctification. Justification by faith rests on the legal provisions of the cross, but it is more than a legal declaration: it enables the believer to be obedient to all the commandments of God.

Robert J. Wieland

1

How Can You Stop Doing Wrong After You Believe in Christ?

The letter flowed in the quaint idiom of an African village teenager for whom English is a precarious second language. But it jolted me, as if my dentist had jabbed a raw nerve. The letter started and ended simply enough:

"Dear Christ's followers: I am a new young Christian. I have [am] faced with problems and I need help. ... Can I know much from you? [Signed] Magara"

But those questions in between were difficult for me to answer, living as I do far from his real world in his remote African village. But I must send him some answer since Jesus Christ is the Saviour of "all men" and expects His ministers to have something helpful to say even to a teenager in an African village. Magara first asks this question:

(1) "The Bible says that if you meet one who is in a bad way, help him. Suppose while I was going on the way, I found someone carrying a pot of *pombe* [native beer]; shall I help him?"

I happen to know a little about African village life. The "one in a bad way" carrying a pot of *pombe* is very likely his aged aunt or grandmother. To her, selling her beer is the only way she knows to get some cash for buying soap or salt. Suppose Magara, the "new young Christian," refuses to have anything to do with her enterprise. "No, dear grandmother; I can no longer help with the 'manufacture or sale of alcoholic ...'" She retorts, "What a fine Christian *you* are—not helping your poor old grandmother!"

The next question is as difficult:

(2) "Suppose I am on the way from the church on the Sabbath, and I find someone carrying a very heavy sack of maize to market; can I help by carrying it?"

This is also very likely a relative, maybe the same grandmother or aged aunt. "No, dear aunt, I am a Christian now and I cannot help you carry your heavy burden *today*. Only tomorrow." You think Magara's questions are easy to answer? Put yourself in the African village, and you'll see they are not!

But the last question almost stumped me, for it crystallizes in microcosm the great struggle between Christ and Satan and perplexes every alert follower of Christ wherever he lives.

(3) "What can one do not to do wrong again when he has believed in Christ?" What does Magara mean by this question?

Magara's village is what the apostle John called "the world" which we are not to love any more. His village may be even more "the world" than the place where you live, even though your "world" may be filled with sex shops and pornographic magazines on your street corner and lurid massage parlor signs beckoning you on your way to town.

Magara doesn't need *Playboy* or *Hustler* in his village, nor does he need to pay money to see temptations in books, magazines, or on a screen. Such vicarious pleasures would be ludicrous there. Many village girls—even professed Christians—are only too ready to put on a show for Magara—the real thing, free, anytime. And he knows very well how enticing are their wiles. Most of his Christian friends have no scruples about not "doing wrong again" after one has "believed in Christ."

The overwhelming impact of nearly a century of Christianity in Africa has drilled into the people the idea that you keep right on sinning after you become a Christian. The only difference now is that you are *saved in* your sins instead of being lost in them, provided you keep your accounts with God up to date by proper confessions in church or to the priest, penances, and attendance at church, especially on Christmas and Easter.

You don't stop being human when you become a Christian, do you? The girls in Magara's village have a coy way of asking him, "OK, you're a Christian now—but you're still you, aren't you, big boy?"

The pastor of one of Africa's largest churches recently lamented in public that over 90 percent of the brides who marched down his cathedral aisle last year were pregnant. And a bishop complained in the newspaper that most of the "big guys" involved in massive embezzlement and corruption are professed Christians. Of course, it is said, you're not expected to stop sinning when you become a Christian! It's *impossible* to stop. Doesn't everybody know that?

But Magara has a conscience that bothers him. He has discovered a pointed question that the Bible asks: "Should we continue to live in sin so that God's grace will increase? Certainly not! We have died to sin—how then can we go on living in it? For surely you know that when we were baptized into union with Christ Jesus, we were baptized into union with his death." Romans 6:1-3, TEV.

Magara has gotten this far in his Bible and he is concerned. He *is* still human—that he knows only too well. Maybe even painfully well. It didn't take long after his baptism for this to sink in. He still has his old sinful nature to contend with. He even discovers something else: evil desire seems enhanced now, and temptations are more alluring than they used to be. And he has heard of the African theologian who has come back from the overseas seminary who openly says that "occasional lapses" into sin are biblical and are "par for the course," that you simply cannot expect to overcome all temptations, and that the best you can hope for is to be a bit more discreet now.

"Occasional lapses"—that's rather elastic, Magara realizes. The interpretation can be according to your individual desires—once a week, maybe even once a day?

According to his letter, Magara dreads these defeats, for they leave him feeling polluted, guilt-ridden, and dissatisfied. Although pastors say that Christ saves you *in* your sins because He has done it all for you and that you can't do other than continue to transgress, Magara would like to know about some "good news" that will do better than that. If Christ can't save you from sinning today, how can you be sure He can resurrect you later on? What kind of future life would there be if "saved" people haven't stopped sinning?

The best "good news" he too often hears is the kind that Bishop Fulton Sheen marketed so enticingly: "One look at [Virgin Mary], and we know that ... because she is without sin, we can become *less sinful*."—*The World's First Love,* (London: Burns and Oates, 1953). p. 16. Emphasis supplied.

Therefore, if this were true, Magara must not raise his expectations too high. The best he can hope for is a tapering off, becoming "less sinful," but always expecting those "occasional lapses" that both Catholic and Protestant teachers say are so inevitable.

The girls, of course, aren't Magara's only problem. He probably liked the *pombe* his grandmother makes so well, for drinking alcoholic beverages has always been his way of life. And since childhood he has also probably been taught to lie, at least to tell white lies. Furthermore, who doesn't "blow his top" and swear when things don't go right? And the temptation to worship money is as real to him as to anybody else in the world.

That is why Magara is pleading, "I need help!"

Do I have some good news for Magara? Yes, I do! It's what the Bible calls "justification by faith." And if Magara can understand it, anybody can.

2

New Testament Justification by Faith: the Kind That Works

I was glad to tell Magara that God's justification is to a sin-sick soul (and that includes all of us!) what a refreshing, cleansing bath is to the body. It is the answer to the deep-felt longing of the human heart to be straightened out, to be put right with God and with His universe. To be out of kilter with all that is pure, right, and just is a terrible feeling. We call it guilt. Guilt destroys peace and hope. We need relief.

Justification may sound like a big, mysterious word, something that lawyers and theologians talk about in dry, dusty books. But Magara soon discovered that the Bible idea of justification is as clear as sunlight. The Today's English Version aptly translates the original word for *justify* as simply being "put right with God." Romans 5:1.

Imagine yourself guilty of a crime. No question about it—you are guilty! You are miserable in your prison cell, dreading the day of sentencing. For you, no sun shines, no flowers bloom, no birds sing. You cannot even smile. No one can comfort you. You feel a million miles in "outer darkness"—away from God and from everyone else whom you have disappointed. All you can feel is "a certain fearful looking for of judgment and fiery indignation." Hebrews 10:27. Any one of us can imagine this misery because we have tasted it often.

Then imagine someone getting up in court with evidence to acquit you. He persuades the prosecutor, the judge, and the jury that there is no evidence of your guilt. The jury acquits you. Then imagine listening to the judge pronounce his decision that all charges against you are dropped, and you hear yourself declared by this court to be innocent. The crowded courtroom erupts in applause, and with a respectful flourish, the bailiff escorts you to the free air and sunshine outside.

This is what justification is like, but it falls far short of what justification is; for in our analogy you were guilty and no amount of "evidence" will change that fact. In the plan of salvation, you are not only "declared right" by the Judge, but you are "put right" in the eyes of the community, and something happens within you too. That is the common, everyday meaning of *justify*—"to be put right." A person acquitted of an accusation of crime is not only "declared right" by the judge, but is "put right," straightened out. In printing, a right-hand margin that is "justified" is made straight, not merely declared straight. And so with you.

If there is an ounce of decency in your guilty soul, when you hear that judge pronounce you innocent and free, your immediate response is a wholehearted choice to be straight from then on, especially if the one who defended you in court did so at his own great personal expense and risk (more about this later).

This imagined courtroom case feebly illustrates the biblical idea of justification by faith. To borrow for a moment the theologians' terms, it is both forensic and effective, both legal and practical. It is not produced by any act or work of our own. "God shows that He Himself is righteous and that He puts right [justifies] everyone who believes in Jesus." Romans 3:26, TEV. Justification is a "free *gift* [that] came upon all men by the sacrifice of one, that is, Christ." Romans 5:18. We are "justified *freely* by His grace through the redemption that is in Christ Jesus." Romans 3:24 (Emphasis supplied). He even "justifieth the ungodly" Romans 4:5, and He accomplishes this mighty feat "through His blood." Ephesians 1:7. It is a delicious experience to know in your inmost soul that "if God is for us, who can be against us? ... Who will accuse God's chosen people? God himself declares them not guilty [justifies them]!" Romans 8:31, 33, TEV.

What Justification Meant in Bible Times

If we don't let theologians and commentators confuse us with difficult terms, Scripture alone will interpret Scripture so we can understand it easily. Hence we propose to lay Bible commentators and the Reformers to one side for the moment and let the Bible itself explain what it means by justification by faith. You will discover that it really matters what one believes regarding justification!

1. The Old Testament meaning of *justify* in its primary sense was neither to make righteous nor to declare righteous, but to recognize

evidence that says a person is righteous. Only in a secondary sense did it mean to declare righteous: "If there be a controversy between men, and they come unto judgment [court], that the judges may judge them; then they shall justify the righteous, and condemn the wicked." Deuteronomy 25:1. It would be absurd for a Hebrew judge to "declare righteous" an accused person unless he had previously recognized evidence to support his innocence. He must never make a snap decision of acquittal or condemnation without first laboriously examining all the available evidence. When the evidence confirms acquittal, he must not blind his eyes to it. He may not follow any subjective feelings on his part, prejudiced one way or the other. The "declaring" righteous is only the public expression of his investigation and recognition of the innocence of the accused.

Solomon asks the Lord to justify "the righteous, to give him according to His righteousness." 1 Kings 8:32. It would be redundant to "declare righteous" one who is already known to be righteous. Here again is the idea of examining evidence and recognizing the accused to be innocent (although, of course, no human soul is innocent before God). "Woe unto them … which justify the wicked for a reward, and take away the righteousness of the righteous from him!" Isaiah 5:22, 23.

Here the meaning of *justify* is examining evidence and declaring what it requires without respect to bribes. Of course, we are not to understand that anyone on earth is innately righteous as he stands before God, or that he can earn any merit. But this law-court language prepares the way for us to grasp the meaning of justification by faith in the New Testament.

2. When we come to the New Testament idea of justification, we see again that its primary sense is recognizing evidence that demands a verdict of acquittal. But a new element is now introduced that is never present in an earthly law court. Something is credited or imputed for righteousness which enables God justly to recognize and declare the guilty person righteous. God must not permit Himself to make snap judgments based on subjective feelings or respect for persons. Like the Hebrew judge, He is bound by rules of evidence.

Let us look at several examples of the New Testament idea of justification: "And all the people that heard him [John], and the publicans, justified God." Luke 7:29. This justifying of God was certainly not an arrogant human assumption of the right to judge

God. It was a simple recognition of evidence which proved that God is righteous.

"By thy words thou shalt be justified, and by thy words thou shalt be condemned." Matthew 12:37. Again, this is far more than a mere declaration of innocence or guilt. Elsewhere, Jesus says that in the judgment the Father will not declare any lost person condemned ("the Father judgeth [condemns] no man," John 5:22); and if anyone does not believe in Him, Jesus said He likewise will refuse to declare his condemnation. See John 12:47, 48. Why? Because the evidence of the sinner's "words" will do the job, and all who observe, including those who are subjects of judgment, will concur in recognizing it. Likewise, the acquittal of the righteous will rest on evidence easily recognized—their "words" demonstrating faith in Christ.

The Sublime Paradox

The new element that comes into the picture is Christ's righteousness which is imputed (or credited) to the guilty person who believes in Him. (See Romans 4:6.) This is no celestial legal trick. If it were a mere maneuver, God could perform His legal manipulations without requiring any faith from the sinner. But it is clear that Christ's righteousness can be imputed to the guilty sinner only if he has faith.

This tells us something. The sinner's faith enables God to do the otherwise impossible—to be just while He justifies the unjust. He creates a sublime paradox, a beautiful arrangement that rests on a legal foundation, but embracing infinitely more than a mere legality. The sinner's faith frees the legal logjam that otherwise would force God to abandon him to death—"the wages of sin"—which he deserves.

Such faith is obviously a magnificent phenomenon, complementary to God's own character of infinite love which provides Christ as our Substitute. It makes possible the beautiful formula of justification *by faith*. Faith is never our saviour, but it does make it possible for Christ's work as Saviour to be effective in our behalf. Our search for the meaning of faith is indeed the treasure hunt of the ages! Abraham's justification by faith is the grand model set before us: "Abraham believed God, and it [his faith] was counted unto him for righteousness. ... To him that worketh not, but believeth on him that justifieth the ungodly, his faith is counted for righteousness. ... Faith was reckoned to Abraham for righteousness." Romans 4:3-9.

Counting or reckoning faith for righteousness is the same "recognition" idea we found in the Old Testament. It is radically different from the Roman Catholic invention of an infused righteousness poured in by the sacraments. Abraham did no ritual works of any kind; no righteousness was poured into him. Rather, his faith was counted for righteousness. Although his faith was not based on human performance, something had indeed happened within Abraham himself. As in the case of all true Christians, Abraham "with the heart" believed "unto righteousness." Romans 10:10. His heart was melted by something extraordinary: he discerned the sacrifice of Christ in his behalf, for he "saw [Christ's day], and was glad." John 8:56. His faith was a heart appreciation of the sacrifice of that "Lamb slain from the foundation of the world." Revelation 13:8. Thus he became the "father" of all sinners "justified by [Christ's] blood." Romans 5:9.

This means that justification *by faith* must be more than a mere declaration of acquittal on the part of God. (It is that, of course; but it is also a reckoning or recognition by God of the sinner's "faith ... for righteousness.") Justification by *faith* therefore goes far beyond a legal declaration, because it is a reconciliation of the sinner's heart, a miracle accomplished by the Holy Spirit who awakens this dynamic faith "which worketh by love." Galatians 5:6. And that working of faith in justification is not to be confused with sanctification—another theological word we will discuss later.

Paul has a grand idea, and we must let him get it across. It is simple and clear, and is not contradictory to our God-given sense of fairness. You don't have to believe a fiction in order to believe in justification by faith. The brilliant idea Paul has is that a sinner's *faith* is "reckoned" for righteousness, and this great idea packs a punch.*

Imagine that you are in Paul's audience. In Romans 3:19 he has shown that all the world is guilty of sin that crucified the Son of God and that no one can be justified by any attempted obedience to the law of God for the simple reason that "all have sinned" by breaking it, and hence they cannot put themselves right. But "all" are "justified ['put right', verse 24, TEV] freely" by the grace of Christ when He shed "His

---

* Note: In this book the phrase "justification by faith" carries a broader meaning than generally understood. Similarly, the phrase "righteousness by faith" includes both justification by faith and sanctification by faith—both gifts of God's grace in His plan to restore sinners to His image.

blood" for us. Something about this sacrifice enables God to "declare His righteousness for the remission of sins that are past." Verse 25. People have often criticized this as illegal, unfair, even immoral. How can a fair God permit a good person's righteousness to be credited to a bad person? Isn't this a legal shenanigan? The kind of trick clever lawyers pull off behind the scenes?

Paul is aware of this charge. He goes on to say that God is just (has a right) to do this for the one who has faith—the one who believes in Jesus. Romans 3:26. Faith becomes the all-important key in this strange but wonderful transaction. The "law ... of works" (Romans 3:27) is useless; what counts now is a new law—"the law of faith." Faith becomes a principle in God's grand economy of salvation.

A Picture of True Justification by Faith

"Is anything not clear?" Paul seems to be asking. "Don't get discouraged; hang on a little longer," we seem to hear him say. It is said that a picture is worth a thousand words, and in chapter 4 we're going to see a picture of justification by faith—Abraham himself. We'd rather see a sermon any day than hear one, and Abraham is Paul's sermon, the supreme example of someone justified by faith. Even a child can understand by looking at the picture.

Abraham is claimed by millions, both Jews and Christians, as their "father," so that he is perhaps the most important man that lived in the era before Christ. But regardless of anyone's genetic claims on Abraham, Paul says, he can be "our father" only if we have his faith. His life experience is our story encapsulated in a fantastic struggle with doubt that went on for decades, while he "against hope believed in hope." Verse 18.

The Lord raised his expectations sky high by promising to make him "a great nation" through which the Messiah was to come, so that in Abraham "shall all families of the earth be blessed." He would have as many children as there are stars in the sky. (See Genesis 12:2, 3; 13:14-16; 15:5, 6.) But what is this thing called faith?

And then the Lord seemed to drop out of sight, leaving the poor man to stagger on for decades with no sign of even one child being born to him. Most everyone else, it seemed, had no trouble having plenty of children, while he, with the tremendous promise ringing in his ears, appeared to be doomed to go childless.

When he left Haran to go to the Promised Land, Abraham, at seventy-five, was getting old and Sarah's hopes for becoming a mother faded with her increasing age. (She was only ten years younger than Abraham.) When Abraham was eighty-six, they tried to solve the problem with a kind of second-wife arrangement whereby Hagar bore Ishmael. But the Lord refused to recognize him as the promised heir, and another long decade ground slowly by with still no sign of a baby conceived by Sarah. See Genesis 16:17. Everything looked hopeless. God was powerful enough—both Abraham and Sarah were convinced of that. The problem was whether He was willing. Where was His love? (We always find it easier to believe in miracles of omnipotence than in divine willingness.)

And then, when Abraham was ninety-nine, something happened. Hebrews tells us that both he and Sarah together had "faith," and the impossible gynecological thing happened; Sarah conceived. There was great rejoicing when little Isaac was born. Such happiness must have been almost too much to endure after decades of hoping against hope with continual disappointments.

But the old hero's trials were not over. When Isaac was about twenty and the father's love for him the most tender and mature, God tested his faith a final time with the most horrendous trial that any mortal saint has ever had to face. He was to offer Isaac as a burnt offering on the hill that should later be crowned with Golgotha's cross.

Again the problem the poor man had to wrestle with was his perception of the character of God. Where was His love? Could Abraham believe when everything seemed to indicate that the Lord was a cruel ogre, as bad as the Canaanites' gods? In the thick darkness of finite sense, could he have faith to anticipate John's declaration that "God is love"?

With the infirmities of old age making the test more excruciatingly painful, Abraham went through it firmly and loyally. He "staggered not at the promise of God through unbelief." Romans 4:20. See also Genesis 22. And thus he well earned the right to that distinctive title by which we sometimes refer to him—"the father of the faithful," that is, of those who are full of faith, who appreciate and trust God's character of love when everything seems to deny it.

In Abraham's life experience was forged for all time the model of justification by faith. The Genesis formula, "He believed in the

Lord; and He counted it [his faith] to him for righteousness," became the cornerstone for Paul's earth-shaking concept of righteousness by faith. See Genesis 15:6 and Romans 4:3-9.

How the "Law of Faith" Works

No one can improve on the way Abraham was "put right." All anyone has to do is to walk in the steps of that faith, which Abraham walked—not in the steps of mere human performance, says Paul, but in the steps of his faith! The "good news" of justification by faith was as valid in Abraham's day as it has ever been.

Like all the rest of us, Abraham was a sinner and deserved what all sinners deserve—death. "The promise ... was not to Abraham ... through the law, but through the righteousness of faith." Romans 4:13.

Please remember: Abraham's faith does not *equal* righteousness; it was *counted* for it. When he "believed God," his faith was neither an intellectual assent to doctrines nor a self-centered grasping for reward. It was not a clever move on his part to ensure for him or his descendents some valuable real estate, that is, the earth. Such "faith" would merely have been a smart yet selfish bargain. Neither was his faith a fire escape from the terrors of hell. That would mark him as merely a knowledgeable opportunist. It was not a trust built on self-centered insecurity.

"With *the heart* man believeth unto righteousness." Romans 10:10. Emphasis supplied. Abraham's faith was a heart-experience, or "heart-work," as earnest people of a former generation used to call it. By his faith Abraham was himself transformed from an enemy of God into a friend of God. He was actually reconciled to God, although he had no works to offer on which to be justified. All he had was faith, and that, Paul adds, while he was as yet uncircumcised. But that was all God asked from him!

But what is this thing called faith?

3

Christ *Did* Something for "Every Man"

Most of us hesitate to respond to junk mail for fear we might get trapped into some kind of obligation. Modern man often says, "I don't want to get involved," whether it's helping with the neighbors' problems, lending to a friend, or even (for many) making a bargain with God. Don't become obligated seems to be sage counsel.

If I let God mind His own business while I tend to mine, have I incurred any obligation to Him? Suppose I decide that the stories about heaven or hell don't faze me, and I choose to go it alone and ignore God. I never pray, never ask Him for anything, and never darken the door of any of His churches. Do I owe Him anything? Assuming their computers are healthy, Macy's department store can't send me a bill if I've bought nothing from them.

The subtle ideas of predestination and its ancillary concepts would probably lead many to assume that they don't owe God anything, if they haven't been signed up for the trip to heaven. Such people have had nothing to do with Him, and He supposedly has had nothing to do with them, except to ignore them. The troubles and disappointments they have had reinforce their assumption that He has written them off. They may have tried praying at some time, but got no answers. They've been on their own all this time, so why do they owe God anything? If an employer pays you no salary, do you owe him any time? The answer is obvious.

Here is where the truth of justification says something to all of us, to "every man": he owes absolutely everything to God, whether or not he thinks he wants to get involved. He has already been paid a big salary and has already purchased a huge package of goods from God;

he is most definitely obligated—to the hilt. And the information that this is so is called "good news." How can this be?

If the Internal Revenue Service informed us that we owe the government a sum equivalent to all our assets, including every last penny we possess, would we call that *good* news? But that is precisely the state of our ledger account with God. So says the New Testament doctrine of justification by faith; and it *is* good news! And it's not that our pie in the sky or life after death is what we owe Him; for we owe Him for everything we possess *now,* all that makes our life enjoyable in *this* world.

How can this be *good* news?

Very simply stated, the gospel discloses the fact that every man would already be in his grave (and a hopeless one at that) if Christ had not first gone there in his place. Our present life itself (forget heaven for a moment) is an undeserved dividend: It is the "salary" we have already received, and even every morsel of food we have ever enjoyed is included in the goods we have "bought." When Scripture insists that "all have sinned," it means that "all" would already have suffered sin's penalty, eternal death, for "the wages of sin is death" (see Romans 3:23; 6:23), the second death.

The fact that we live is evidence that we have already been reprieved. Someone else has received our deserved "wages" and has given us life instead. For every man, the ledger account of sin has already been balanced, whether or not he realizes it. God has already *legally* imputed to his credit the doing and dying of Another who is righteous. This perfect life and sinless character is the substance of Christ's righteousness. The Bible emphatically declares that the purely legal (or forensic) justification was made not only for those who believe, but for *all* men: "All have sinned, and come short of the glory of God; being justified freely by his grace through the redemption that is in Christ Jesus." Romans 3:23, 24. The New English Bible sharpens the focus: "All alike have sinned, … and *all* are justified by God's free grace alone." He offers His grace freely to all without distinction. If the grace is free, it cannot rest on any merit or work performed by us. "All the world … [has] become guilty before God" (Romans 3:19), and by His death Christ effects for all the world a free legal justification: "God was in Christ, reconciling the *world* unto himself, not imputing their trespasses unto them." 2 Corinthians 5:19. "The grace of God hath appeared for the salvation of *all* men," as Titus 2:11 reads in the margin of some Bibles. "As by the offence of one judgment came upon all men to condemnation; even so by the righteousness of one the free gift came upon *all men* unto justification of life." Romans 5:18.

The good news is that the work has already been accomplished! God has no chip on His shoulder against anyone, no matter how sinful he is. One died for *all*. Christ did something for every man, woman, and child in the world. He has "brought *life* and immortality to light through the gospel." 2 Timothy 1:10. For all men He has "brought life"; but for those who believe, He has also "brought ... immortality."

What "Every Man" Owes to Christ

It's a mind-boggling truth when you grasp its real dimensions: Every human being draws his next breath solely because "one died" in his place. Aside from the sacrifice of Christ we would all be in our graves, and whether or not we profess to serve the Lord makes no difference. "To the death of Christ we owe even this earthly life. The bread we eat is the purchase of His broken body. The water we drink is bought by His spilled blood. Never one, saint or sinner, eats his daily food, but he is nourished by the body and the blood of Christ. The cross of Calvary is stamped on every loaf. It is reflected in every water spring. All this Christ has taught in appointing the emblems of His great sacrifice. The light shining from that Communion service in the upper chamber makes sacred the provisions for our daily life."— Ellen G. White, *The Desire of Ages,* p. 660.

The "saint" partakes of communion, by faith recognizing the grace of his Lord; the "sinner" may likewise partake of it, but without faith, "not discerning the Lord's body." 1 Corinthians 11:29. This, in fact, is the basic difference between saints and sinners.

When this discernment dawned on the mind of Paul, it worked an immense transformation in him. And the same transformation is worked in you and me if we "discern" the Lord's body and believe: "The love of Christ constraineth us; because we thus judge, that if one died for all, then were all dead [that is, all would be dead]: and that He died for all, that they which live should not [that is, will find it impossible] henceforth [to] live unto themselves, but unto Him which died for them, and rose again." 2 Corinthians 5:14, 15.

In this passage Paul is talking about how people think he may have lost his mind. Why devote himself so untiringly to the service of Christ? Why not settle down in a comfortable villa by the Mediterranean and enjoy a well-earned retirement? Why keep on and on in those long missionary journeys, stoned, imprisoned, beaten, shipwrecked, maligned, "in deaths oft"?

The answer he gave was that he believed himself to be "justified by faith." "One" had died in his place. The simple equation he reasoned out is valid for "all men." If it is true, then "all men" have nothing they can rightfully call their own, not even their next breath. All that they enjoy is theirs by the grace of a Saviour—cars, houses, careers, friends, money, love, a happy marriage, sex, reputation, what have you. And faith henceforth constrains those who believe and appreciate His gift of grace to live not for themselves but for Him who died for them and rose again. This motivation becomes the most powerful force at work in humanity.

"The love of Christ" does the work, not Paul. He is no super-human, heroic soul made of sterner stuff than all the rest of us. He is simply an ordinary weak sinner who has exercised an extraordinary faith in the One who died for "all." He saw something, that's all—something that most of us have been too blind to see. He saw the truth of justification *by faith* which makes the sinner to be obedient to the holy law of God and captivates his heart for eternity.

No one can possibly truly obey, except through this way. And when anyone has this faith, he cannot possibly *live in disobedience*, for his faith is an energizing force that "works." Formerly he was alienated from God, for we "were God's enemies, but he made us his friends through the death of his Son." Romans 5:10, TEV. We have been "justified by his blood." Romans 3:9. The death of His Son *makes* us His friends. John 15:15. If justification by faith changes God's enemies into His friends, it must be extremely powerful!

John the Baptist saw this truth when he said, "No one can have anything unless God gives it to him." John 3:27, TEV. This is the basis for true human love. It is the solution to the vexing social problems that poison our modern lives. Love, the "sweet mystery of life" soon turns bitter, unless such love is gratefully accepted in faith as the gift of Heaven. To take what God has not given is the sin of fornication or adultery, the sin of despising what God has given. Marriage is not ours; it is part of our infinite debt.

Paul's insight is "good news" because God's grace enables the Christian to put an end to all fornication, infidelity, cheating in marriage, and broken homes. It is foreign to the spirit of the gospel: "You know that your bodies are parts of the body of Christ. Shall I take a part of Christ's body and make it part of the body of a prostitute? Impossible! Or perhaps you don't know that the man who joins his body to a prostitute becomes physically one with her? The Scripture says quite plainly, 'The two will become one body.' ...

"Avoid immorality. Any other sin a man commits does not affect his body; but the man who is guilty of sexual immorality sins against his own body. Don't you know that your body is the temple of the Holy Spirit, who lives in you and who was given to you by God? You do not belong to yourselves but to God; He bought you for a price." 1 Corinthians 6:15-20, TEV.

Since "faith ... worketh by love," it works purity which brings happiness with no remorse: "Your life must be controlled by love, just as Christ loved us and gave his life for us. ... Since you are God's people, it is not right that any matters of sexual immorality or indecency or greed should even be mentioned among you. Nor is it fitting for you to use language which is obscene, profane, or vulgar. Rather you should give thanks to God." Ephesians 5:2-4, TEV.

The amazing thing is that all this is not our hard work of self-denial; it is what *faith* does! The dynamic power is in the gospel, not in us. In our next chapter we must look still more closely to see what such faith is. It is still a largely undiscovered world to be explored.

4

Faith: What Is the Real Thing?

One wonders if anything has ever been talked about so much and yet understood so little as what faith is. Yet it is an essential ingredient of the three-word formula, "righteousness by faith," which has been discussed so much, that some think they are weary of hearing about it.

But since New Testament faith itself is a world largely undiscovered, New Testament righteousness by faith is also a realm of truth largely awaiting exploration. While it is destined to enlighten the earth with glory, Christ assures us that at the present time we are actually "poor, blind, and naked" in understanding it, while we have imagined ourselves "rich and increased with goods." Discovering the fabulous secrets of the gospel is a more fascinating search than diving for Spanish gold in sunken treasure.

One reason so many find the topic righteousness by faith dull, as presented in the gospel story, is that the dynamic New Testament idea of faith is rarely seen. It once "turned the world upside down" (Acts 17:6), according to the enemies of the gospel; and if the true idea ever gets unwrapped again, the results will be the same.

But the common "evangelical" idea of faith can never turn the world upside down. This is because it is basically self-seeking; yet millions of Christians naively suppose that this egocentric preoccupation is perfectly proper. Instead of self-seeking with worldly, materialistic objectives in mind, you merely transfer your concern to real estate in heaven, and presto, your self-seeking becomes a holy quest. Faith is then conceived of as your trust that you will get the great reward you seek. Is this not the same root of self-seeking, only on a higher, disguised spiritual plane?

New Testament faith is always something far greater than egocentric trust. The best known verse in the Bible discloses Jesus' own definition of faith: "God so loved the world, that He gave his only begotten Son, that whosoever believeth in him should not perish, but have everlasting life." John 3:16.

God does the loving; God does the giving; *we* do the believing. (Remember: believing and having faith is the *same* word in the original language.) Our faith (believing) is dependent on His loving and giving. Such faith could not even exist if there were no revelation of God's love first; everything depends on that loving and giving on the part of God. Christ's definition of faith here is seen to be our heart appreciation of God's loving us and His giving of His Son for us. Such faith cannot be egocentric in nature.

Paul's powerful idea of faith is built on the foundation of Jesus' definition: "*With the heart* man believeth unto righteousness." Romans 10:10. The revelation of God's love must come first, for no man can believe without it. Then "faith ... worketh *by love*." Galatians 5:6. Because faith is not a superficial, sentimental emotion, it grips human hearts at its deepest level of affection and profound feeling. A human being without this response is a human being without faith, the ultimate state of every unbelieving soul. Believing "with the heart" leads to the awakening of love by a revelation of love; yet Paul dares not say faith is the same thing as love. The experience of genuine faith leads to genuine love. Love is a gift from outside man's selfish nature.

But, wonder of wonders, that cold sinful heart can be awakened to *appreciate* God's love when it is revealed at a place called Calvary. And *that* is Paul's idea of faith. God so loved that He gave the gift of Christ, "whom God hath set forth to be a propitiation through faith in his blood." Romans 3:25. We may have become blasé by the familiar phraseology, but it evoked a magnificent response in human hearts when Paul wrote it.

How the Cross Exposed the Dimensions of God's Love

Consider what had happened when Jesus came to earth. The Son of God had become one "with us," closer and dearer than a brother. All our human, long-dormant capacities for affection, devotion, and aspiration were aroused as never before, because God created man in His image. It was not that we loved Jesus as a human being (in His weakness we could love Him as a human being), but we could also worship Him; we could adore Him without the guilt of idolatry. He was a man, but He was also "God with us." Matthew 1:23. Never had earth known such a Person. Our love for Him in His weakness was mingled with awe and reverence for His divinity.

And then as did His disciples, we saw Him murdered, broken, bleeding. We saw His blood flow freely, yet we had an indefinable conviction that we were somehow involved in His murder, because we realized that our sinful mind is "enmity against God." From this point of view, even we, in the person of His disciples had been angry with Him because He loved us so much that He would not save Himself or seek political power and material riches. Then we had proved false to Him and forsook Him. One of us had even denied Him, and another had betrayed Him—all of us: We were hiding, or silent, at His trial.

Never had the sight of blood so moved human hearts as when we saw Him die like that. It was indescribable. Hope of reward in heaven, fear of punishment in hell, all egocentric concern were alike cast out by this magnificent new passion of "faith in his blood."

This was the faith in Paul's justification by faith. When he spoke of "being now justified by his blood" (Romans 5:9), it was in this context: "Peradventure for a good man some would even dare to die [such as Alcestis being willing to die for her husband, the good, handsome Admetus in the well-known Greek legend], but God commendeth his love toward us, in that, while we were yet sinners [enemies, verse 10] Christ died for us." Romans 5:8. Astounding! This was the message of love that turned the ancient world upside down.

Two Greek words in the New Testament are essential to understanding the gospel. The first is love [*agape*], self-sacrificing love, and the second is our word which is dependent on it—*faith.*

The Key Word of the Bible: Agape

As a noun or verb, *agape* (love) occurs some 300 times in the New Testament. Its most thrilling use is John's sublime equation, the high point of the New Testament: "God is love [*agape*]." 1 John 4:8. There is a "breadth, and length, and depth, and height" (Ephesians 3:18) of *agape* seen only in the cross, a love as much greater than our best human love as a mountain towers over a grain of sand.

We could never invent such love as led Jesus to His cross, for it is unworldly, something that could come only from above. It does not depend on the beauty or goodness of its object, as does our natural human love. It creates value in its otherwise worthless object, whereas our love weakly depends on the value of its object.

Agape does not seek to climb up higher, but is willing to step down lower, "even [to] the death of the cross" (Philippians 2:8), the equivalent of the second death, a death that includes hell within it. Such love is the wonder of earth and heaven because the death of the cross was universally regarded as the curse of God, the utter and final hiding of His face. And yet the Father's love was equal to the Son's, for He "so loved that he gave." The Son gave Himself to endure the horror of that hell for us.

The Human Response
That God's Agape Made Possible

The second key word *pistis*, "faith," occurs in the New Testament as a noun or verb some 500 times. It is by no means the equivalent of trust, although of course a trust is included in it. But when Paul spoke of trust, he always used a different word. (We will give more attention to this later.) When we superficially define New Testament faith as trust, we imply a basic foundation of insecurity which creates egocentric, fearful concern. We trust our bank because we are afraid to hide our money under the mattress. We trust the police because we are afraid to walk the streets without knowing they are around. We trust the government because we fear the alternative—anarchy. To say that we trust Christ for our salvation can be far short of the magnificent faith of the apostles, because such trust can still be tied to our egocentric radius of selfish concern.

Such trust may be ever so good and justifiable in the light of sinful man's natural self-centeredness. But it is not New Testament faith. This phenomenon which was repeatedly spoken of as *"the* faith" must be understood, or we can never grasp what happened in the time of the apostles. The content of their faith depended on a clear appreciation of the content of *agape.* Destroy or weaken the idea of *agape,* and you automatically destroy or weaken the inner content of faith. And since justification by faith is the only way we can be "put right with God," it is no surprise that Satan has cleverly worked to corrupt the meaning of *agape* so that he could corrupt the meaning of faith, and thus do away with the true gospel.

This clever maneuver on his part can be traced in the history of the early church, and is the reason why there are so many conflicting concepts of righteousness by faith.

In our next chapter we must uncover the exciting story of how Satan stole away from sincere Christian people the truth of God's love and the truth of New Testament faith.

5

How the Enemy Stole Our Faith

The weapon Satan used to corrupt the idea of *agape* was the pagan notion of the natural immortality of the soul. This idea was almost universal, infiltrating even Judaism, at times. The New Testament idea in contrast is clear-cut: man is by nature mortal and is unconscious in death. Immortality can come only through Christ and can be conferred only at the resurrection from the dead or by experiencing what the Bible calls translation, both of which occur at Christ's second coming.

The notion that man possesses inherent immortality requires the righteous to go to heaven directly at death or, as some would have it, to a half-way station known as purgatory. This teaching also requires that the wicked go directly at death to a place of endless life in incessant torment or torture worse than anything the German Gestapo could invent. It can readily be seen that this doctrine not only bypasses any need for a resurrection from the dead, but also seriously distorts the character of God into what is virtually a deity guilty of sadism.

What is even more serious, this pagan notion neatly destroys the real meaning of the cross of Christ, because it corrupts the idea of the love demonstrated there. If this be true, then obviously Christ could not die on the cross, and God could not truly love the world so much that He gave Him for us—He only lent Him. And Christ could not have died for us a true death, the equivalent of the "second death." See Revelation 2:11; 20:14. From this point of view, He merely suffered mental and physical agony as have many soldiers mortally wounded in war, many of whom have suffered for even longer periods of time than Jesus did when He died on the cross. The idea is that Christ only *lent* Himself to us briefly.

This pagan notion of natural immortality has Christ assuring the thief on the cross that both he and Christ would together share a great reward that very day (the comma placed before the word *today* is inserted by translators and has no place in the original Greek). Luke 23:42. While it is true that up to this point Jesus was conscious of ultimate victory, this was not the end or the full measure of His sufferings and death for us. After the episode with the repentant thief, darkness enveloped the cross and Jesus entered the terrible experience of the hiding of His Father's face—something He had never experienced before. It was this that is described as His tasting "death for every man." Hebrews 2:9.

The Real Meaning of Death

This "death" was not what we superficially assume it to be. What we call death is not the real thing, for the Bible calls it "sleep." See John 11:11-14 and 1 Thessalonians 4:15-17. Jesus "tasted" the *second death* "for every man," the death in which there is no cheering light of hope at all. It's as though every cell of your body, soul, and mind is agonizingly crushed by the horror of a great despair. And for Christ on His cross there was no blessed unconsciousness to block out the full realization of this horrible darkness.

No man since time began has ever felt that full weight of condemnation and despair except our Lord. It was the full weight of the "curse" of God that Paul quoting Moses said rested on "every one that hangeth on a tree" (see Galatians 3:13 and Deuteronomy 21:22, 23), although no other crucified person ever felt it to the full. This is what Isaiah means when he says that Christ "poured out his soul unto death." Isaiah 53:12.

Can we imagine the horror of a great darkness forever, the aloneness, forsakenness, or eternal separation from the Father, the utter ruin, shame, and humiliation that being lost involves? No, mercifully, we can not comprehend it, for the reason that Another has already "tasted" it for us, drinking the bitter cup in our stead. We would perish if we did taste it. But this is what He endured for us. He was no actor wailing His lines on a stage, pretending what He didn't truly feel. When He cried out, "My God, my God, why hast thou forsaken me?" (Matthew 27:46) He meant every syllable of it. Not the pain of nails in His hands and feet, but the horror of that eternal forsakenness killed Him. It was caused by the guilt laid upon Him—the guilt of the accumulated sin of the world.

The point is that "in this was manifested the love [*agape*] of God toward us." "Herein is love [*agape*], not that we loved God, but that he loved us, and sent his Son to be the propitiation for our sins." 1 John 4:9, 10. Untainted by the Greek notion of natural immortality, the apostles understood what had happened on the cross. There, the "breadth, and length, and depth, and height" of "the [*agape*] of Christ which passeth knowledge" was displayed for the world and the universe to see. See Ephesians 3:18, 19.

With such clear vision, the apostles also sensed a mighty power tugging at their human hearts, a force truly phenomenal: "The [*agape*] of Christ constraineth us [controls us, NASB]; because we thus judge, that if one died for all, then were all dead: and that he died for all, that they which live should not henceforth live unto themselves [that is, they will find it impossible to do so], but unto him which died for them, and rose again." 2 Corinthians 5:14, 15. Just seeing what that love was resulted in this "constraint" going to work in the heart immediately. Faith was a heart-appreciation of God's *agape* love.

How the Apostles' Faith Becomes Ours

We don't have to be one of the early apostles to "see" with eyes what they saw. Through the Word, the Holy Spirit makes it all come alive for us now. See Galatians 3:1. Our alienated hearts are likewise reconciled to God by faith, and this means that we are also reconciled to God's law at the same time, for our natural "enmity against God" consists in not being "subject to the law of God." Romans 8:7. And since "love is the fulfilling of the law" (Romans 13:10), the "faith which worketh by love" (Galatians 5:6) immediately produces obedience to all the commandments of God, including the widely downtrodden Sabbath commandment.

In the time of the apostles, be sure that sensuality, materialism, the love of money and luxury, living for one's own self were as powerful temptations as they are today! Our pitiful struggles to overcome these temptations they would have considered nonsense. What they did know was that faith *worked*, like a bomb exploding. We think it so hard to follow Christ, to sacrifice for Him; they would have pitied our lack of understanding. What they had was New Testament justification by faith, which turned the world upside down and crucified the world unto them. See Galatians 6:14.

Can you guess why Satan would want to eliminate that constraint of love? This was behind his efforts in the early Christian era to distort and confuse this idea of *agape* until Christ had to sorrowfully say to the church of Ephesus (the early church), "Thou hast left thy first love [*agape*]." Revelation 2:4. Many of the church fathers lost its meaning, so much so that Plotinus in the third century rejected the idea that God is *agape* and boldly declared Him to be the Hellenistic idea of self-centered love based on natural immortality. So entrenched had the apostasy from love become by the fifth century, that Augustine, father of Medieval Romanism, synthesized the conflicting New Testament and Hellenistic ideas of love into what he called *caritas,* which became the basis of medieval Romanist doctrine.

Contrary to Augustine's intentions, it produced a deplorable system of salvation by meritorious works because it was egocentric in nature.

The worst tragedy came later. Protestantism generally inherited Augustine's idea and perpetuated within itself the same principle of self-centeredness. Thus the idea of justification by faith commonly held by the Reformers contained the seed of its own eventual corruption. It is no wonder that Revelation addresses the Reformation church of Sardis as the one who has "a name that thou livest, and art dead." Revelation 3:1.

Luther, however, in the sixteenth century rejected the pagan notion of natural immortality, and consequently began to break down Augustine's synthesis and to restore New Testament *agape*. Luther's grasp of the biblical truth of the nature of man enabled him at times to have a clear understanding of justification by faith. But Calvin and other Reformers clung to the pagan-papal doctrine, as did Luther's colleagues and descendants. With their idea of the love of God thus crippled, it is easy to see how their idea of faith was likewise maimed. They were never able to escape that tethered radius of a self-centered faith and get back to the grand New Testament idea.

Their concern was always overshadowed by their sense of insecurity and fear. "How can I be sure *I* can escape the tortures of hell? How can I be sure *I* will get a reward in heaven?" were of necessity questions uppermost in their minds. It was not their fault;

they were grand men. They had simply inherited a false doctrine of the nature of man. Their ideas of justification by faith were always tinctured by self-concern and a horrible fear of eternal torture and torment; and lurking beneath the surface was the idea of a vengeful, angry God who hardly deserved the name of Father. The apostle John saw how "perfect [agape] casteth out fear" (1 John 4:18), but this they could not really comprehend; obsessed as they were by their doctrine of natural immortality, they could only work toward degrading their concept of Christ's sacrifice. Their egocentric search for security was unavoidable. They could never break through the mists to see New Testament righteousness by faith in all its majestic grandeur.

So confused were many of the Calvinists that they distorted the New Testament to make it teach that an arbitrary God predestined one to be saved regardless of his unbelief, and another to be lost regardless of his faith. For all practical purposes, this brand of Calvinism degraded justification by faith into justification by arbitrary predestination. Such broken cisterns are hardly a pure source of the water of life! This does not impugn the sincerity or devotion of the Reformers of previous centuries. The kindest thing to say is that they were sincerely but unknowingly confused by their inheritance of a pagan-papal error.

The Reformers Who Almost Succeeded

The Wesleys almost broke through the confusion into the light. They rejected the Calvinist form of predestination, and their concept of the character of God was immeasurably superior. But they were still confused by the notion of natural immortality which in subtle ways beneath the surface still worked to distort for them the full truth of the gospel and to hold them to some extent bound by egocentric concern.

It may be said of them all what Hebrews says of earlier generations, that God has "provided some better thing for us" (Hebrews 11:40) in the end of time. "The road the righteous travel is like the sunrise, getting brighter and brighter until daylight has come." Proverbs 4:28, TEV. But God honored "the angel of the church" of the Reformers, for He promised, "I will give him the morning star." Revelation 2:28.

Scattered here and there in the centuries since Luther were a few individuals who saw clearly and spoke boldly enough to reject the pagan doctrine of natural immortality. The New Testament doctrine of life only in Christ—conditional immortality—was often derided by its numerous opponents as Mortalism. Bryan Ball says of some of its adherents in England: "In 1646 Richard Overton was sent to the Tower for having written a book which explained the Mortalist viewpoint, and in 1658 Thomas Hall listed Mortalism as one of the 'devilish' errors of the time. It ... had been condemned as heretical in the Forty-two Articles of Religion of 1553."—*The English Connection,* p. 159.

In the last days there must be a full recovery of "the everlasting gospel" of justification by faith as both Abraham and Paul experienced it. And it must be a vast multitude of "every nation, and kindred, and tongue, and people" who say "with a loud voice, Fear God, and give glory to him; for the hour of his judgment is come: and worship him that made heaven and earth." Revelation 14:6, 7. It is impossible to worship Him "in spirit and in truth" (see John 4:23), unless His character of true love is clearly perceived as free from pagan-papal distortion. And "the hour of his judgment" is not the hour when in sadistic vengeance He condemns the world. He expressly said He would not do that. See John 5:22; 12:47, 48. It is the hour when He Himself is acquitted and vindicated, when the mists of distortion and misrepresentation concerning Him are at last blown away by the full truth.

Here is predicted the full recovery of New Testament *agape,* which alone makes the everlasting gospel to come into its own. Significantly, the fruitage of this revival of the gospel is the development of a people who are characterized as "they that keep the commandments of God, and the faith of Jesus." Revelation 14:12. Only "[*agape*] is the fulfilling of the law" (Romans 13:10); and here again New Testament faith is seen as a human heart-appreciation of the cross. Keeping the commandments for the saints is no fear-inspired search for security or assurance. It is the automatic expression of their appreciation of Calvary. They simply glory "in the cross of our Lord Jesus Christ, by whom the world is crucified unto" them, and they "unto the world." Galatians 6:14. They know they live only because "One died for all." New Testament faith sees the grave as one's only rightfully earned reward. Everything else that we have is ours only by grace. And in this faith is a guarantee of happiness and the end of repining, jealousy, selfishness. They cannot exist in company with faith! And obedience becomes as natural as daybreak following night.

The people of the last days who are "saints" in God's sight feel the grateful appreciation that moved Elizabeth Clephane to write her hymn "Beneath the Cross of Jesus":

There lies beneath its shadow,
    But on the farther side,
The darkness of an awful grave
    That gapes both deep and wide;
And there between us stands the cross
    Two arms outstretched to save,
Like a watchman set to guard the way
    From that eternal grave.

Upon the cross of Jesus
    Mine eye at times can see
The very dying form of One
    Who suffered there for me;
And from my smitten heart with tears
    Two wonders I confess:
The wonders of redeeming love,
    And my unworthiness.

I take, O cross, thy shadow
    For my abiding place;
I ask no other sunshine than
    The sunshine of His face;
Content to let the world go by,
    To know no gain nor loss,
My sinful self my only shame,
    My glory all the cross!

Elizabeth Clephane could have served well as Paul's singing evangelist! She saw what he saw: "faith which worketh by love" kills every form of human selfishness at its root. A believing heart responds not a whit less than to say with Isaac Watts: "Love so amazing, so divine, Demands my life, my soul, my all!" This is justification by faith. And nothing less can be worthy of the name.

6

More About This Explosive Word, *Faith*

S ince faith is the key word in understanding the power of the gospel to transform our lives, we must look at it a little more closely. If the New Testament idea is not clear, the entire subject of righteousness by faith will be confusing to us, and boring as well.

I am sure some are asking the questions, "What about the many Christian writers and speakers who have defined faith as mere trust? Could they be wrong? And doesn't the author of Hebrews, in his classic definition in chapter 11, define faith as trust?"

The apostle Paul never uses the noun *faith* or the verb *to believe* with the meaning of trust as we use that word today. The most common verb used for *trust* is *elpizo,* which means "to hope." Here are a few examples: "In him shall the Gentiles trust." Romans 15:12. "I trust to see you in my journey," says the apostle. Romans 15:24. "I trust in the Lord Jesus to send Timothy," he adds. Philippians 2:19. "We trust in the living God." 1 Timothy 4:10. "A widow ... trusteth in God." 1 Timothy 5:5. In each of these and other passages, it is obvious that "hope" is what is meant. In none of them does Paul use the word *pisteuo,* to believe or to have faith.

When the Jews said of Christ on His cross, "He trusted in God; let Him deliver him" (Matthew 27:43), the word used is *peitho,* the common everyday word for *trust.* The same word is used in the following places: "How hard ... for them that trust in riches" (Mark 10:24); "I trust ... in God" 2 Corinthians 1:9; "I will put my trust in Him" (Hebrews 2:13). Here the meaning is clearly equivalent to that of our ordinary word *trust,* which means "to have confidence." Why is *pisteuo,* (believe) never used by Paul to express such confidence or trust?

Paul *appears* to make two exceptions, but they are not exceptions. We shall examine them. Neither, if properly translated, expresses *man's* trust in God, but *God's* trust in man! It is interesting to study these uses of *pisteuo,* which appear on the surface to require the translation of "trust" or "entrusted." In each instance the subject is the gospel being entrusted to the care and ministry of Paul himself. No English word can properly convey the sublime thought contained in what Paul is saying. His use *of pisteuo* here must borrow its luster from its usage elsewhere in the New Testament—that of a heart-appreciation of the love of God revealed at the cross. Two passages from Paul, and one from Luke, must be considered:

First Thessalonians 2:4: "We speak as men approved by God to be entrusted with the gospel." NIV. Translators obsessed with the natural immortality idea have failed to see the depth of meaning in this passage. It is not by accident that Paul uses this word *pisteuo,* which is so freighted with the content of human appreciation for the cross of Christ. What he says is this: "We speak as men approved by God to be appreciative of the gospel," or "as men approved by God to be enamored with or captivated by the gospel." Again this pregnant word *pisteuo* must be understood in the light of Christ's own use of it in John 3:16.

First Timothy 1:11: "The glorious gospel of the blessed God, which He entrusted [*episteuthen*] to me." NIV. Here we have the same idea again linked with an appreciation of the "glorious gospel." Is Paul so arrogant as to claim that this "glorious gospel" was "entrusted" to him as a kind of exclusive franchise? Hardly. The point he is making in all Christian humility (see his context) is that the Lord found in him one who had a heart-appreciation of the good news. He was captivated by it. This was his qualification for proclaiming the gospel—he loved it. And this is the thought he expresses in the next verse: "Our Lord ... considered me faithful," that is, full of faith in the sense of an appreciation for His grace, for this reason "appointing me to his service." While he was "once a blasphemer," he was "shown mercy" because he acted "in ignorance and unbelief," that is, non-faith. In those dark days his hard heart knew no contrite appreciation of what the cross meant. But "the grace of our Lord was poured out on me abundantly, along with the faith and love [*agape*] that are in

Christ Jesus." 1 Timothy 1:13, 14, NIV. In neither of these passages is *pisteuo* used with any semblance of egocentric trust.

Luke 16:12: "If you have not been trustworthy with someone else's property, who will give you [*pisteusei*] of your own?" NIV. Here is an instance where *pisteuo* has the meaning of trust, but its usage is not related to righteousness by faith or the content of the gospel. Jesus was here using the word in its common everyday meaning, as understood by the people of His day before the tremendous disclosure of the cross event. Both words, *agape* and *faith*, were immeasurably enriched with meaning as a result of the crucifixion, so much so that they virtually took on new meaning. God's love revealed on Calvary invested the word *agape* with a meaning far beyond itself; and likewise its dependent word, *faith,* acquired a meaning never before comprehended. It was as if new terminology had to be invented.

Thus the passage in Luke is not an excuse for restricting *faith* in Paul's letters. We have no alternative but to view his use of the word *faith* in the light of the cross.

The assumed definition of faith in Hebrews next deserves our attention: "Faith is the substance of things hoped for, the evidence of things not seen." Hebrews 11:1. Or, "faith is being sure of what we hope for and certain of what we do not see. This is what the ancients were commended for." Hebrews 11:2, 3, NIV. This passage definitely does not define faith as an egocentric trust. Several factors need to be considered:

1. The immediate context is discussing righteousness by faith. (See Hebrews 10:38: "Now the just shall live by faith."). Unless this one passage is out of harmony with Paul's voluminous discussions elsewhere of justification by faith, the meaning of faith here must be the same as we find in all his epistles. Even if Paul were not the author of Hebrews, we should not expect to find a contradiction because the same Holy Spirit who inspired the writer of Hebrews inspired Paul.

2. It is possible to hope for things "not seen" without the necessity of a self-centered motivation being involved. We can hope for the vindication of God's cause without our hope growing out of our own sense of personal insecurity. True faith includes a desire for the honor and glory of Christ. Our concern is not that *we* shall wear a crown in our Father's house, but that we see *Him* crowned King of kings and Lord of lords.

3. If Paul should indeed be the author of Hebrews (as good authorities say is possible), we may have here a profound insight into his high regard for faith, an insight complementary to his frequent use of the word in his other letters. After discussing in the close of chapter 10 the efficacy of faith in the experience of justification by faith, in Hebrews 11:1 he says in effect: "This phenomenon that we know as faith, this heart-moving appreciation we feel for the sacrifice of the Son of God which has so transformed our lives, *this* faith experience is the guarantee or down payment that guarantees all the promises of God will be fulfilled in due course. This human faith which is complementary to God's divine *agape* is itself a miracle, and thus it is the 'substance' underlying all miracles we yet expect." This verse, if this is correct, is not intended to be understood as a definition of faith.

4. The author proceeds throughout chapter 11 to cite examples of Old Testament heroes whose motivation of faith was anything but self-centered. Noah became "heir of the righteousness which is by faith" (Hebrews 11:7), but the fear which moved him was not *phobos,* a craven self-centered dread, but a godly reverence (*eulabeia*). The "father" of all who believe, Abraham, demonstrated in type the glorious meaning of faith when he "offered up Isaac" as God offered up His only-begotten Son. See Hebrews 11:17. Here was a miniature reflection of John 3:16. And so all the "elders" of ancient times, weak and imperfect as they were, in some way partook of this phenomenon of New Testament faith, for like Abraham they "saw" Christ's day and were glad. They somehow sensed that the Lamb had been slain from the foundation of the world, and though none saw it as crystal clear as did the apostles, they all had some concept of the cross, and their hearts were deeply moved by it. *This* was their faith.

But does not verse 6 declare that faith is a grasping for reward? "Without faith it is impossible to please Him: for he that cometh to God must believe that He is, and that He is a rewarder of them that diligently seek Him." Of the versions in common use the KJV alone indicates for us which English words are supplied in that they are printed in italics to show that they are not in the original language. The literal Greek reads as follows: "Without faith impossible [it is] to please Him, for he that comes to God must believe that He is; and to those seeking Him, a rewarder He becomes." Note that in the KJV the word "that" is a supplied word; the Greek here does not support the idea that faith is a self-centered seeking for reward.

With this key, one can unlock treasures of truth in the Bible. Faith is not a set of doctrines or a creed assented to intellectually. As the matrix and type are related to each other, so God's prodigious love is related to our human faith. The sacrifice of Christ elicits from otherwise hopeless sinners its complementary heart response—"faith in his blood." Abraham knew it; tears rolled down his cheeks as he "believed God, and [his faith] was counted unto him for righteousness." Romans 4:3. It moved his soul even to the sacrifice of his son on Mount Moriah.

Perhaps the most sobering statement in Paul's writings is this: "Whatsoever is not of [this] faith is sin." Romans 14:23. Only with the heart can one "believe unto righteousness." Romans 10:10. If salvation were by works, multitudes could qualify themselves, although none would be fit to enter heaven; but salvation is by faith alone, and Jesus foresaw that "when the Son of man cometh" He would find precious few who have it. Luke 18:8.

Why? Because "iniquity shall abound, [and] the love [*agape*] of many shall wax cold"? Matthew 24:12. "Iniquity" here is *anomia,* hatred of God's law of *agape* ("*agape* is the fulfilling of the law," Romans 13:10). The greatest sin of all time is that which kept ancient Israel out of their Promised Land—unbelief (see Hebrews 3:19), hardheartedness, lack of appreciation of the cross where the Prince of glory was to die for us.

Speaking of Israel's unbelief, the author of Hebrews pleads with us, "Let us therefore fear, lest ... any of you should seem to come short." Hebrews 4:1. While fear is not the proper gospel motivation, an absence of gospel faith should cause us to fear, because this fatal unbelief is sure to rule the human heart where the gospel is not understood. Unbelief carries its own built-in incapacity for sensibility. It is to "crucify ... the Son of God afresh, and put Him to an open shame" without realizing what we do. Hebrews 6:6.

One thoughtful writer has offered us a virtual definition of faith that is in perfect harmony with the New Testament concept: "You may say that you believe in Jesus, when you have an appreciation of the cost of salvation. You may make this claim, when you feel that Jesus died for you on the cruel cross of Calvary; when you have an intelligent, understanding faith that His death makes it possible for you to cease from sin, and to perfect a righteous character through the grace of God, bestowed upon you as the purchase of Christ's blood."—Ellen G. White, *Review and Herald,* July 24, 1888.

Charles Wesley understood it. He prayed:

> O for a heart to praise my God
>   A heart from sin set free,
> A heart that always feels Thy blood,
>   So freely shed for me.

It would not be amiss for us to pray with John Newton, "The feeling heart, the melting eye, the humble mind, bestow."

When our Lord said that "iniquity [*anomia*] shall abound" in the last days, (Matthew 24:12), He could have been referring to the subtle inroads of antichrist's thinking into our latter-day consciousness. He could have been referring to a counterfeit justification by faith that does not produce obedience to all of God's commandments, and thus works *anomia.* Such a counterfeit lacks the vital ingredient of *agape,* and, of course, genuine New Testament faith. The overmastering deception of the ages is religion without *agape,* without faith, employing all the proper vocabulary, but minus its essential content, the great "grain" robbery of spiritual nourishment. If the righteousness-by-faith diet we feed on is bereft of its vitamins and minerals, the resultant *anomia* is a spiritual anemia.

But our Lord gives the encouraging promise that "this gospel of the kingdom shall be preached in all the world" before the end comes. Matthew 24:14. Since the divine administration of the gospel comes from the high-priestly ministry of Christ Himself, we must seek to understand how His present work in the heavenly sanctuary is the true avenue through which the Holy Spirit today ministers to His believing children the benefits of justification by faith. In this light, the ultimate counterfeit can be distinguished from the genuine.

In a later chapter we shall search for the link that binds "this gospel of the kingdom" to the closing work of Christ as High Priest in the most holy apartment of the heavenly sanctuary and exposes the counterfeit.

But our next task must be to discover what sanctification is and whether it comes by faith or by works, or perhaps by both.

7

You Can't Crash If You Keep on Believing!

Not an iota of human works is involved in justification by faith. And of course it would be criminal to try to distort faith so one could talk about "salvation by faith," when in reality he means salvation by works.

We are not saved by faith *and* works, but by faith that works. And it is not exaggeration to say that we are saved by faith *alone;* that is simple, pure New Testament teaching. Only it is not a "dead" faith. So long as God's love is seen clearly, undistorted by pagan-papal falsehood, the resultant faith will "work" and in genuine love will produce everlasting obedience to all of God's commandments. This is how the gospel "is the power of God for the salvation of everyone who believes." Romans 1:16, NIV.

But the question now is this: After one has been justified by faith, is he then on his own? Is he like a plane that, having become airborne, must keep up its speed or crash? This idea has struck fear to many. Is God standing back in the shadows with His divine arms folded, saying something like this? "I got you started with justification; now it's up to you to keep going with your own sanctification. I hope you make it, but most people don't. Good luck!"

Where does one draw that hairline distinction between justification by faith and sanctification? Is sanctification by works, by our own hard, agonizing effort? Or is it partly by faith and partly by works?

Since commentators and theologians have sometimes seen justification by faith out of focus, it is reasonable to assume that it is equally possible for them to misunderstand sanctification. If we can search the New Testament to discover its idea of justification, perhaps we can also find there what sanctification is. The two may be distinct, but they are never separate.

Sanctification Is God's Work

Anybody who is justified by New Testament faith is automatically in the process of sanctification. He never has to change gears from salvation by faith to salvation by works. "As ye have therefore received Christ Jesus the Lord, so walk ye in Him, ... stablished in *the faith*." Colossians 2:6, 7. By his expression "*the* faith" Paul does not mean a creed or a set of doctrines, but the phenomenon of a heart-appreciation of Christ's cross. The method remains the same: *by faith.*

"Being justified by faith, ... we have access by faith into this grace wherein we stand." Or perhaps the same passage can be rendered more clearly: "Now that we have been put right with God through faith, we have peace with God through our Lord Jesus Christ. He has brought us by faith into this experience of God's grace, in which we now live." Romans 5:1, 2, TEV. In sanctification, it is the Lord who brings us along our way, as He did in justification. Faith *keeps on* working by love, always in the present tense.

In no way does the Lord leave us to fly on our own, to keep up our speed or crash. Sanctification is never by works; neither is it a mixture of faith and works in the sense of self-motivated efforts to chalk up merit so we can earn a reward. Clearly, Christ told Paul that He was sending him to open people's eyes and "turn them from darkness to light, ... so that they may receive forgiveness of sins and a place among those who are *sanctified by faith in* Me." Acts 26:18, NIV. We do not read anywhere in the New Testament that it is our job to sanctify ourselves. Instead, we are "sanctified by the Holy Spirit." Romans 5:16, NIV. Jesus prays the Father to sanctify us (see John 17:17); and Christ also sanctifies and cleanses His church (see Ephesians 5:26).

It is all summed up in Paul's comprehensive statement: *"May God himself, the God of peace, sanctify you through and through, ...* blameless at the coming of our Lord Jesus Christ. The One who calls you is faithful, and *He* will do it." 1 Thessalonians 5:23, NIV.

The Lord doesn't give up easily. "He who began a good work in you will carry it on to completion until the day of Christ Jesus." Philippians 1:6, NIV. *This work that He does is sanctification.*

Part of the Galatian error was that some supposed that they had to keep up their speed themselves, or crash: "O foolish Galatians!

Who has bewitched you, before whose eyes Jesus Christ was publicly portrayed as crucified? Let me ask you only this: Did you receive the Spirit by works of the law, or by hearing with faith? Are you so foolish? Having begun with the Spirit, are you now ending with the flesh? ... Does He who supplies the Spirit to you and works miracles among you do so by works of law, or by hearing with faith?" Galatians 3:1-3, RSV. (Please note: "Works of law," or ritual works, is a correct translation here, and is not the same as true obedience to the law. "Works" are self-centered efforts to win a reward.)

Human effort is not the means of sanctification. Christ justifies us, and the Holy Spirit sanctifies us; but that which arouses faith in the beginning—Christ crucified—keeps faith active throughout. It is the "believing" that enables the Holy Spirit to do the work, all the way along.

Does this mean we do nothing? Is this "quietism," the heresy of letting the Lord do everything while we virtually slide into heaven free of effort? While it is true that the Lord does the sanctifying as long as we do the believing, we *do* have a part, and a very important one.

As in justification, our part is to have faith and such faith is not self-centered "works of law." It is a continuing sense of the constraint of the love of Christ that motivates us to live not for ourselves but for Him who died for us and rose again. This is how we are "sanctified by faith" in Christ. Acts 26:18.

What Makes Our Battle an Easy One

While the Holy Spirit indeed does the work, our part is to "let" Him do it, and that is important. Our "carnal mind" is constantly fighting Him. If we don't consent for Him to sanctify us, He is blocked and frustrated. *"Let* this mind be in you, which was also in Christ Jesus." Philippians 2:5. *"Let* the peace of Christ rule in your hearts." *"Let* the word of Christ dwell in you richly." Colossians 3:15, 16, NIV. The power of choice is ours, and what the Lord does in us is always contingent on our choice to let Him do it. It was a wise writer who said this: "What you need to understand is the true force of the will. This is the governing power in the nature of man, the power of decision, or of choice. Everything depends on the right action of the will. The power of choice God has given to men; it is theirs to exercise. You cannot change your hearts, you cannot of yourself give to God its affections; but you can *choose* to serve Him. You can give Him your will; He will then work in you to will and to do according to His good pleasure."—Ellen G. White, *Steps to Christ,* p. 47.

In Rwanda near what is now Mugonero, a man-eating lion had been troubling the African villagers. This was terrible; no one felt secure. The villagers came to Dr. John Sturgess to ask him to bring his gun and shoot the offender.

Dr. Sturgess took his 7mm Mauser with the hair trigger and went with the guide. They walked a long distance, when finally the guide said, "Here is where we last saw the lion."

The missionary reached in his pocket for some bullets, and discovered to his horror that he had left them at the mission.

"Quick," he urged the guide, "hurry back and fetch the ammunition for me. I'll wait for you here."

There was a log nearby, and he sat down to wait, then dozed off. He was awakened by a rustling noise in the grass just in time to see the lion facing him.

He realized his gun was useless. To run would be sure suicide. As the lion took a step toward him, the missionary took a trembling step toward him. The lion got into springing position, ready.

Dr. Sturgess realized in a flash that he must do something quickly. Throwing down his useless gun, he took another step toward his enemy. Seeing the beast hesitate for a fraction of a second, he decided to turn things right around backward from usual, and charge the lion. On he came, shouting, waving his arms wildly, looking the lion in the eye and yelling, "Go away, GO! GO!"

The beast was taken completely by surprise. How dare this puny, two-legged creature come at *him,* yelling and screaming as if *he* were the king of the forest? He was so shocked that he turned tail and ran.

Our "enemy the devil prowls around like a roaring lion" (1 Peter 5:8, NIV), but we are the boss. We have been given the power of choice, and Christ has given "all men" liberty to exercise it. A firm, decided choice makes us indeed king of Satan's forest, for if we "resist the devil, ... he will flee." James 4:7, NIV. By "the right action of the will," exercising this God-given authority, "you will tread upon the lion and the cobra; you will trample the great lion and the serpent." Psalm 91:13, NIV.

"I Choose to Say No!"

Thousands of people have quit smoking through accepting the simple formula, "I choose not to smoke." When temptation assails us, our part is to choose not to yield. Then the Holy Spirit is free to go into action. No matter if your will is weak, you are still the boss. The tempter can never force you to do wrong against your will.

"No man can be forced to transgress. His own consent must be first gained; the soul must purpose the sinful act before passion can dominate over reason or iniquity triumph over conscience. Temptation, however strong, is never an excuse for sin."—Ellen G. White, *Testimonies,* vol. 5, p. 177.

The "good news" of sanctification by faith is beautifully expressed in the New International Version's rendering of Paul's letter to Titus: "For the grace of God that brings salvation has appeared to all men. It teaches us to say 'No' to ungodliness and worldly passions, and to live self-controlled, upright and godly lives in this present age, while we wait for the blessed hope—the glorious appearing of our great God and Saviour, Jesus Christ, who gave Himself for us to redeem us from all wickedness and to purify for Himself a people that are His very own, eager to do what is good." Titus 2:11-14.

Do you know how to pronounce that word "No!" to temptation? "The grace of God" will teach you! It teaches you to be the boss, the king; and none of the enemy's most alluring temptations can stand up against that word "No!" which expresses our "right action of the will."

And how does "the grace of God" succeed in teaching us backward mortals such a marvelous skill? By providing the dual motivation of (a) an appreciation of how Christ "gave Himself for us," and (b) the delightful anticipation of letting Him "purify for Himself a people" ready to honor Him at His "glorious appearing." It works!

Is choosing hard? When you fall in love with someone, is it hard to "forsake all others" and "cleave" to that loved one? The constraint of the love of Christ makes all the allurements of the world seem as pale as a street light glowing in comparison with the pure brilliance of the sun. Also when we are yoked up with Christ, we find that He bears the weight.

This is what it means to "live by the Spirit" or, to "walk in the Spirit." It is a constant choosing to say "No!" to temptation, and "Yes!" to the Holy Spirit. He never forsakes us, night or day, twenty-four hours a day. He is the One called to come and sit down beside us; He is with us constantly. "Whether you turn to the right or to the left," it is His voice that you hear "behind you, saying, 'This is the way; walk in it.'" Isaiah 30:21, NIV.

This response of faith is not salvation by works, not even one percent; "we walk by faith." 2 Corinthians 5:7. As we respond by faith to the good news of justification, so we now respond by the same faith to the prompting of the Spirit. See Colossians 2:6. We *let* this mind be in us which was in Christ Jesus. See Philippians 2:5. When sorely tempted, He cried out, "Not as I will, but as Thou wilt. ... Thy will be done." Matthew 26:39-42. Thus He exercised His own power of choice. "I came down from heaven, not to do Mine own will, but the will of Him that sent Me." John 6:38. Oh, it was indeed a terrible struggle; but He gained the victory as we are to gain it—by "the right action of the will."

He will never will for us or excuse us from exercising our own power of choice, even though we read that "it is God who works in you to will and to act according to His good purpose." Philippians 2:13, NIV. Since the Lord gives the Holy Spirit to tell us, "This is the way," and also gives us the power of response, He works "in" us "to will." But this never bypasses our own volition, nor does He over-whelm it. Not all the angels in heaven tugging together in our behalf can release us from making our choice pro or con, nor can all the fallen angels in hell force us to make a wrong choice.

Since we can choose to "let this mind be in [us], which was also in Christ Jesus," does this mean that the believer is now saving himself by his own efforts? Is surrendering to the guidance of the Holy Spirit a do-it-yourself religion in which we pull ourselves up by our own bootstraps? Never! Although we cannot save ourselves even one percent, we can *let* our Lord save us 100 percent!

Power Steering Illustrates the Gospel

If we make the right choices, we "walk in the Spirit." We "let" Christ's "mind" be in us, in the sense of motivation. It's like using power steering to drive a huge truck. No way can you turn those great front wheels yourself; but if the engine is running, your choice to turn right or left is all that is needed—the slightest pressure on the steering wheel activates the power-steering pump to do all the work. Paul didn't have power steering in his day, but he understood the secret of sanctification by faith: "So I say, live by the Spirit, and you will not gratify the desires of the sinful nature. For the sinful nature desires what is contrary to the Spirit, and the Spirit [desires] what is contrary to the sinful nature. They are in conflict with each other, so that you do not [cannot] do what you want." Galatians 5:16, 17, NIV.

So, it's "good news" again! The "power source" is the Holy Spirit. Give Him your will, make your choice to walk in His way, and (according to Paul's Greek) you *cannot* be overcome by the desires of your "sinful nature," however strong they may be or however long you have walked in evil habits. The reason is simple enough: the Holy Spirit is stronger than the flesh, just as light is stronger than darkness and love is stronger than hate.

It seems hard for us humans to grasp the truth that we have such a Saviour! He is real! We are not left on our own! He gives us our wings, and if we believe with New Testament faith, we *cannot* crash.

8

The Holy Spirit's Work Is Constant Good News

Does that seem surprising to you? That the Holy Spirit's work is more good news? Most people believe that God seems to be a kind of celestial Killjoy who prohibits everything enjoyable. If you keep on doing what you like to do, you'll be lost; so the only way to be saved is to do what you don't like to do, which is uphill climbing and hard work all the way. Worse yet, trying to keep from doing what you like to do is sheer torture. And that is supposed to be the "faith of Jesus."

There is nothing "good" in news like that! The Bible gives a completely different idea:

1. *The Holy Spirit does all the hard work.* Like my African friend, we are aware of the tremendous pressure that our sinful human nature continually puts on us. But the "good news" is that we are not left to battle alone with these forces that would drag us down to ruin and death. The Holy Spirit does the battling, and our part is to choose to "let" Him do so. The astounding truth in Paul's message here deserves more of our attention: "What I say is this: let the Spirit direct your lives, and you will not satisfy the desires of the human nature. For what our human nature wants is opposed to what the Spirit wants, and what the Spirit wants is opposed to what our human nature wants. These two are enemies, and this means that you cannot do what you want to do." Galatians 5:16, 17, TEV.

"What you want to do" is obviously what your sinful human nature prompts you to do, for Paul goes on to say that "human nature ... shows itself in immoral, filthy, and indecent actions. ... People ... are envious, get drunk, have orgies, and do other things like these." Galatians 5:19-21. These things are what you as a Spirit-filled

Christian "cannot do" even though your sinful nature "wants to do" them, because Someone stronger than your sinful nature—the Holy Spirit—has won the battle.

It's like a guarantee: "You *will not* satisfy the desires of the human nature." The Holy Spirit is an enemy to sin, and *He* does the fighting. It's like injecting medicine into your bloodstream to fight malarial parasites that cause illness. Once you "let" the anti-malarial drug into your veins, it immediately goes to work, for it is the enemy of the parasites. *You* don't fight the malaria; in fact, there is nothing you can do to oppose it. The strongest man gets laid low by the disease unless he has help of some kind from outside. The medicine does all the work.

So, says Paul, "*let* the Spirit direct your lives," like you "let" that powerful anti-disease medicine into your veins. Your consent is what is necessary; then *He* goes to work.

On the other hand, if you believe the "flesh" (one's sinful nature) is stronger than the Holy Spirit, then you see this passage as terribly bad news. (Of course, needless to say, if there were no Holy Spirit to help us, we would be hopelessly in captivity to the clamors of the "flesh.") But it says that the Spirit works, striving against the clamors of the sinful nature. Now, if it were true that the Holy Spirit can be beaten in the struggle and the flesh wins out, then of course you "cannot do" the *good* things you would like to do. This is the common idea many people have—the Holy Spirit can be beaten. And there couldn't be worse news than that.

If you believe the Holy Spirit is stronger than the flesh, then this emerges as fabulously good news. We are all aware of those constant "desires of the flesh and of the mind" that keep surfacing and seeking to win our consent. And since we have already fulfilled them, putting up resistance to them is that much more difficult. See Ephesians 2:2, 3. But since the Holy Spirit is at work to strive against the flesh, striving "contrary" to it, He wins the battle, and we "cannot do" the evil things that we are prompted to do, so long as we choose to let Him fight our battles for us. There is a sort of noblesse oblige operating in us now, and we are actually kept from yielding to sin.

This is indeed the dynamic good news Paul is trying to give us. Paul absolutely will not give us any bad news! The New English Bible points up his message more directly: "I mean this: if you are guided by the Spirit you will not fulfil the desires of your lower nature. That nature sets its desires against the Spirit, while the Spirit fights against it. They are in conflict with one another so that what you will to do you cannot do." Galatians 5:16, 17, NEB.

The Revised Standard Version is even more explicit: "The desires of the flesh are against the Spirit, and the desires of the Spirit are against the flesh; for these are opposed to each other, to prevent you from doing what you would [that is, gratify the desires of the flesh]."

Christ through the Holy Spirit does the striving! As Christ says in His prayer to the Father in John 17:1, 2, He has authority or power "over all flesh." His Vicar on earth, the Holy Spirit, is always stronger than the desires of our selfish, sinful nature. The first step for us, therefore, is to simply believe this truth.

The Today's English Version clarifies a detail in a previously quoted verse that is important: "What I say is this: let the Spirit direct your lives, and you will not satisfy the desires of the [sinful] human nature." Galatians 5:16.

Maybe this is completely different to what you've been taught. You may have never understood that the gospel is such good news. But I must convey to you what the Bible actually teaches. And I don't know of anything elsewhere in the Bible that contradicts the good news Paul gives us here.

2. *The Holy Spirit is sent to everyone who believes the "good news."* Jesus promised: "I will ask the Father, and He will give you another Helper, who will stay with you forever. He is the [Holy] Spirit, who reveals the truth about God. The world cannot receive Him, because it cannot see Him or know Him. But you know Him, because He remains with you and is in you." John 14:16, 17, TEV.

This word *Helper* is *Comforter* in the King James Version. Neither word is an adequate translation of what Jesus said—*parakletos*, which was His way of introducing the Holy Spirit to us. The world "cannot see Him or know Him," but still "he remains with you and is in you." The word *parakletos* means two things: (a) He stays with us all the way (*para*, as in parallel). Two railroad tracks that are parallel stay together all the way, and thus the Holy Spirit "will stay with you forever." (b) He is called *kletos*, from *kaleo* to call. He is sent to us from the Father in place of Christ in our hour of need. Thus He is the true Vicar of the Son of God, or if you please, Christ's Vice-president. He is "given" to us; He is ours.

Again, that's "good news."

But isn't it a hard job to remember all you are supposed to remember and to stay on the right path? No, the Holy Spirit takes care of all these problems.

3. *He constantly reminds you of what you need to know and shows you the right path.* He is as patient and persistent with you as if you were the only person He had to take care of on earth. In fact, He is *infinitely* patient, for the simple reason that He is infinite. No teacher ever coached a pupil through his training as faithfully as the Spirit coaches you. Jesus said: "The Helper, the Holy Spirit, whom the Father will send in my name, will teach you everything and make you remember all that I have told you." John 14:26, TEV.

How could you go wrong with help like that, unless, of course, you choose not to "let" Him help you? He *makes* us "remember all" that Christ taught us in His Word. The Old Testament also teaches this same "good news": "The Lord is compassionate, and when you cry to Him for help, He will answer you. … He himself will be there to teach you, and you will not have to search for Him any more. If you wander off the road to the right or the left, you will hear His voice behind you saying, 'Here is the road. Follow it.'" Isaiah 30:19-21, TEV.

Of course, when you read "the Lord," it means God. The Father, the Son, and the Holy Spirit are one. The "voice" we hear is that of the Holy Spirit, Christ's Vicar. There is no possibility that we can lose the path, with Him staying beside us all the way like that.

If we fall into sin while we have help like that, it must be for one of two reasons: either we have rebelled against the Helper Himself, or we don't understand and believe the "good news." The latter is the problem with untold numbers of sincere people. They think they know and believe; and consequently when they fall, they think there is no power in the gospel or that the Lord has reneged on what He promised to do. Or, what may almost be worse, they think that they aren't "cut out" to be Christians, that God has somehow predestined them to be lost. The real problem is they have never grasped how *good* the "good news" of the gospel is.

The only sensible thing is for us to be modest and humble in estimating our understanding of the gospel. Those who think they know it all are cautioned by the Lord, "You say, 'I am rich and well off; I have all I need.' But you do not know how miserable and pitiful you are! You are poor, naked, and blind." Revelation 3:17, TEV. The Bible suggests a good prayer for us to pray: "Lord, I believe; help Thou mine unbelief." Mark 9:24. That's the safest prayer any of us can pray.

But suppose you make mistakes—does the Holy Spirit write you off? Many think so. Their idea is that His love and loyalty are as thin as their own, so that at the least mistake on our part He takes advantage of the opportunity to abandon us. This is why they think it is so easy to sin and so hard to follow Christ.

I don't find in the Bible that the Holy Spirit is anxious at all to leave us. The Father sent Him on a job to "stay with you forever," and He means to do just that. If you persistently and determinedly beat Him off, you *can* commit what Jesus called the sin against the Holy Spirit; but even then it's not He who has forsaken you, but you who have forsaken Him.

Suppose one has already made mistakes after he has decided to follow Christ. What does the Spirit do now? He shifts gears and has another work to do for us:

4. *He gives the gift of repentance.* There are three distinct things He does, and each is tremendous good news:

(a) Jesus said, "It is expedient for you that I go away: for if I go not away, the Comforter will not come unto you; but if I depart, I will send him unto you. And when He is come, He will reprove [convict] the world of sin." John 16:7, 8.

At first thought, this may not seem to be such good news. Isn't the conviction of sin a painful experience? Yes. This is the feeling of hurting, of pollution, of shame, of alienation from God. But on second thought, it's the best good news one can think of. Suppose your body had no nerves to feel the sense of pain. That's what happens when one contracts leprosy. The nerves are deadened or destroyed so that the patient feels no pain, even if pricked with a pin or seared with a hot iron. Lepers have their fingers chewed off by rats while they sleep at night or lose them easily in accidents. Our sense of pain is a tremendous asset. If the Holy Spirit did not do His work of painfully convicting us of sin, we would be insensible to our own self-destruction, for sin always destroys.

How does He convict us of sin? Jesus explains how it happens: "He will reprove [convict] the world of sin, ... *because they believe not on Me."* John 16:8, 9. The real problem with sin is not the doing of the bad things, but the root that produces it. Not believing is that root sin of "unbelief." (Remember, in the New Testament, to have faith and to believe is the same word.) One of the clearest definitions of sin in the Bible is this: "Whatsoever is not of faith is sin." Romans 14:23. No one has ever fallen into sin except when the real reason was unbelief. And if a person believes in Christ in the sense of appreciating His love and righteousness, the result in the life is automatic: righteousness, because "we through the Spirit wait for the hope of righteousness by faith." Galatians 5:5. All unrighteousness, therefore, is the fruit of unbelief. The Holy Spirit puts His finger on the sore spot.

(b) "And when He is come, He will [convict] the world of ... righteousness, ... because I go to My Father, and ye see Me no more." John 16:8-10. Christ was glorified by the Father because He had finished the work He was given to do—developing perfect righteousness in His humanity. In His absence, the Holy Spirit convicts the world of that finished work, for Christ has gone to the Father with that perfect righteousness.

We are by nature so vain that we imagine ourselves to be pretty good people. Our natural sinfulness has blinded us. Have you ever heard an unconverted person boast that he is as good as some people are who go to church?

Our laundered linen hanging on the line looks white until a fresh snowfall shows up its ugly grayness by comparison. Christ's personal presence in this world nearly two thousand years ago reproved His contemporaries of righteousness, because for the first time in history, in contrast to themselves, human beings saw what a character of true love really is. When they saw the revelation of their own selfishness, many were so angered that they cried out, "Crucify Him!" But those who believed were transformed to be like Him in character.

But now Jesus is gone. We see Him no more. So the Holy Spirit does for us that which we could never do for ourselves: He convicts "every man" of an ideal of righteousness, a standard set for him personally by the character of the Son of God. "Every man" can in this way see the contrast between what he is and what he ought to be—and what he can be in Christ. This is a special work of the Holy Spirit! The conviction is more real and His work more efficient for us than if Jesus Himself were our neighbor living next door. And remember, you don't get one eight-billionth part of His attention, even though there are more than eight billion people on earth. Being infinite, He gives us each one as much attention as if we were the only person He has to work with.

This conviction of sin is not to show us up, to make us feel condemned. Not at all: "God sent not his Son into the world to condemn the world; but that the world through Him might be saved." John 3:17. Maybe this threefold look at what the Holy Spirit does to help us is new to you; but if so, consider the surpassing "good news" that the next item contains:

(c) "And when He [the Holy Spirit] is come, He will reprove [convict] the world ... of judgment, because the prince of this world is judged [condemned]." John 16:8-11. The one who is condemned is not you, but Satan! It's a delicious, exhilarating conviction that the Holy Spirit gives: your worst enemy is defeated. Jesus explained Himself further: "Now is the judgment of this world: now shall the prince of this world be cast out." John 12:37. The one who has tormented you all your life, dwarfed your spirit, made you feel inferior and hopeless is thrown out.

Everyone Needs the Thrill of Winning

I remember how once in Kenya I saw a black mamba, one of the deadliest snakes in Africa, heading straight for me. Fortunately I had a club, and I let him have it. The Lord promises, "You will trample down lions and snakes, fierce lions and poisonous snakes." Psalm 91:13, TEV. The sense of exhilaration I felt when I killed that snake was indescribable. Everyone who believes in the Saviour is to share the high spirits of triumph over man's primeval enemy, Satan; and that joy is not "pie in the sky by and by," but something to be known now. Winning in sports is nothing compared to winning in this contest.

Another Gift of the Holy Spirit

Repentance is not something we can generate within ourselves at will: "Him [Christ] hath God exalted with His right hand to be a Prince and a Saviour, for to give repentance to Israel, and forgiveness of sins." Acts 5:31.

As a gift, repentance is worth more than any money could be, for it provides the only avenue of escape from our inward prison, which we detest. It is a supernaturally endowed hatred of sin and a corresponding love for righteousness. Automatically, this produces a change in the life. Again, it is not a work that *you* perform. The Holy Spirit does it in you. Your job again is to "let" Him do it, to "let" Him give His gift. Don't push Him away.

The original New Testament word for forgiveness does not mean a mere pardon, as though God blinks His eye at our sin and excuses it the way you excuse someone for stepping on your toe. The word means "taking away" the sin. God's forgiveness is powerful.

This is why repentance and forgiveness are so closely tied together. A truly repenting person can be freely forgiven by God because the repenting person now hates the sin itself, and therefore the sin is actually gone. Because Christ "gave himself for our sins" (Galatians 1:4), they are rightfully His, and we have no right to hang on to them. Anyone who clings to his sins is robbing Christ of what He bought with His blood.

And where does Christ put those sins He takes away? "You will trample our sins underfoot and send them to the bottom of the sea!" Micah 7:19, TEV.

Any brand of justification by faith that does not include genuine forgiveness as remission of sins and salvation *from* sin is a counterfeit. It is not the New Testament kind.

But New Testament justification by faith never produces pride or fanaticism. He who remembers Christ's cross can have no "holier-than-thou" spirit. He is always aware that he has not one iota of righteousness himself. He knows his weakness, how prone he is to respond to temptation, how easily he can fall. His loyalty to Christ is not a self-centered desire for a reward in heaven but a heartfelt longing to live to the honor and glory of His crucified Redeemer. He has found something to be concerned about that is vastly greater than his own personal security or "acceptance" with God. Like a bride who is concerned for her husband's honor, the believer is caught up in the most thrilling motivation human hearts can ever know—sympathy with Christ in His closing work of atonement.

Where the Reformation Failed

The Protestant Reformers were mightily used of God. But like men chained in dungeon darkness, some could not emerge into the full glory of noonday sunshine all at once. Their extreme view of justification by faith as a purely legal declaration with no change in the life had begun to produce bad fruit by the eighteenth century. Count Zinzendorf explained this belief to John Wesley: "We spit out all self-denial; we tread it underfoot. As believers, we do everything that we wish, and nothing beyond. We laugh at all mortification. No purification precedes perfect love."—John Wesley, *Journal*, vol. 2, p. 490.

Wesley, as a true Protestant, protested against the idea that there is no purification in justification by faith. This brought him into conflict with some who had brought disgrace on the Reformation. One of his assistants, John Nelson, tells of a clash he had: "I met one of them, the other day, so drunk that he could not keep the cart-road. I asked him what he thought of himself now, if death were to seize him in that wretched condition. He said that 'he was not afraid to die, for he was as his Saviour would have him to be; and if He would have him to be holy, He would make him so; but he was a poor sinner, and he hoped to be so to eternity.' He said, 'You and John Wesley are enemies of the Lamb; for you want people to be holy here. I will not offer to save myself, like you Pharisees.'"—Thomas Jackson, *The Lines of Early Methodists* (1870 ed.), vol. 1, p. 140. Quoted by W. E. Sangster in *The Path to Perfection* (New York: Abingdon-Cokesbury 1943), p. 101, 102.

The drunk was wrong! "Without holiness no one will see the Lord." Hebrews 12:14, NIV. It is not that we are to seek holiness selfishly, fearing that the Lord is reluctant to grant it to us. Rather, He is eager to confer it upon us, and we only need to "let" the Holy Spirit impart His gift to us. What He starts He will finish as we continue to consent. He will persevere until He has a people of whom He can say, "They are without fault before the throne of God." "Here are they that keep the commandments of God, and the faith of Jesus." Revelation 14:5, 12.

9

What "Looking Unto Jesus" Means

Once in a while someone claims that he or she has had a glimpse of the Virgin Mary or has seen Jesus in a dream, but the overwhelming majority of us never have such a privilege. We just plod along dreamless and visionless.

Yet we are urged to "fix our eyes on Jesus, the Author and Perfecter of our faith." Hebrews 12:2, NIV. And this command is frequent: "Behold the Lamb of God" (John 1:29); "Look unto Me, and be ye saved, all the ends of the earth" (Isaiah 45:22). We are constantly being told to "keep our eyes on Jesus." How do you look?

"Seeing" an invisible God has always been a problem to man. Ancient peoples felt they had to have images to which they could look and bow down. How otherwise could they "see" an unseen deity? Many even today feel they need images, or at least pictures, to help them visualize Jesus or Mary or the saints or the cross.

The author of Hebrews says, "We see Jesus, who was made a little lower than the angels for the suffering of death, ... that He by the grace of God should taste death for every man." Hebrews 2:9. His point is that we "see" Him in the Bible. The Holy Spirit has the mysterious ability to make the Word come alive in our mind's eye. In fact, through His vicegerent we can be in a sense closer to Christ than were His apostles two thousand years ago when they walked and talked with Jesus personally. See John 16:8, 10. Christ's portrait is etched in the Bible with startling realism and impressed on our minds and hearts with four-dimensional reality.

But often Christ's picture has been blurred in our mind's eye. As an enemy has confused our idea of *agape* and faith, so he has painted over the Scripture portrait of Christ with an unattractive, effeminate counterfeit that conveys an impression of fraud. This is why countless people are sincerely frustrated in their desire to fall in love with Christ. They have inherited a false concept of Him, which awakens no genuine response of sympathy or fellowship in their human hearts. It's as hard or harder than trying to fall in love with George Washington from contemplating his picture on a dollar bill.

How can one possibly relate to an anemic "Christ" with doleful, pious eyes in a stained glass window? You are told that He is God in the flesh. But He seems so remote that any flesh-and-blood point of contact is as alien to us as if He were a man living on the moon. Try as you may, you can't feel a dynamic attraction for Him.

The Problem: False Concepts Innocently Inherited

New Testament believers saw something in Christ that His enemy has tried to plaster over. People need to know that it's not their fault that they don't know how to love Him truly. False concepts which they have innocently inherited are the hindrance. We are as capable of the same heart-thrill of genuine affection for Him as were His apostles. The result of such affection—something infinitely beyond the most gripping love affair one can imagine. And it never turns to ashes, for it lasts forever. You never have to pull yourself up by your bootstraps to try to be good. There's something between you and Christ that does it.

That something is not your tedious job to initiate or even to maintain. Whoever heard of a person truly in love having to *work* to maintain the relationship? The sight, even the memory, of the beloved does it. If effort is necessary, it is usually in the direction of restraining our expressions of love.

In saying this I am not trying to drag faith in Christ down to a sentimental level. I am only trying to point out that constant exhortations to get up earlier in the morning and put forth more effort to maintain a relationship with Christ are often a form of do-it-yourself religion, a subtle kind of legalism that can flourish only where the true Christ of the Bible has been plastered over by the enemy's counterfeit. The problem is invariably a false christ who has not truly "come in the flesh," to quote the apostle John who knew Him so well: "This is how you can recognize the Spirit of God: Every spirit that acknowledges that Jesus Christ has come in the flesh is from God, but every spirit that does not acknowledge [that Jesus has come in the flesh] is not from God. This is the spirit of the antichrist, which you have heard is coming and even now is already in the world." 1 John 4:2, 3, NIV.

Today's English Version makes that last sentence a little clearer: "Anyone who denies this about Jesus does not have the Spirit from God. The spirit that he has is from the Enemy of Christ."

The word translated "flesh" is *sarx,* a term that refers to the fallen, sinful nature of all descendents of Adam, a term never used of Adam's nature before his fall. John's point is that Christ took our fallen nature.

Any "Christ" who did not truly "come in the flesh" is as remote from us and from our human needs as a spaceman on this earth is from a remote planet. He is the "Enemy of Christ," but not openly such, of course. The word *antichrist* means one who arrogates the place of Christ while actually opposed to Him. It's the nearest that John's language could come to a "counterfeit Christ." A hoax has been foisted on an unsuspecting world—and on the church. It has stalled the spiritual development of a people who long ere this should have grown up "into him who is the head, into Christ" to the place where their sympathy and affection for Him are like that of a bride for her husband. The lack of such devotion for Christ is a sure sign that the counterfeit is present somehow.

Christ's bride is caught in the vise grip of worldly materialism and the endless allurements to self-centeredness, which the Enemy has become so skillful at devising. She can never find the strength to wrench herself free from these things until the counterfeit antichrist is unmasked for what he is and the Christ of the New Testament stands revealed in all His genuine appeal to human hearts.

Christ: Fully God and Fully Man

"Looking unto Jesus" establishes contact with Him more effectually than transmitting electronic command impulses through radio contact with a planetary spacecraft. Most people who say they believe in Christ seldom have trouble seeing Him as divine. Their problem is seeing Him as fully human as well. Unless they can appreciate the full dimensions of His divine-human repertory of temptations, sufferings, and sacrifice, they can experience no bond of heart-union with Him. Hence Christ's Enemy has sought to cut the bond that binds Him to our true human nature. This clever maneuver has become a highly sophisticated accomplishment in our day.

Roman Catholic dogma, quite extrabiblical, proclaims that Christ was born of what is called Mary's "immaculate conception." The idea is that Mary, Jesus' mother, was miraculously wiped clean from every taint of "original sin" at the moment of her conception, so that she was unable thereafter to sin in thought, word, or deed. This superhuman advantage made her "the mother of God" with virtually holy flesh. Since she herself was thus cut off from the stream of fallen humanity, she was enabled to endow her Son with her same kind of holy flesh, different from all other human beings, including Adam in his fallen state.

Since the only kind of flesh there is in the world is our fallen, sinful flesh, this teaching effectively declares that Jesus did *not* "come in the flesh." There is a serious element of fraud in such a "Christ," for the Bible claims that Jesus "has been tempted in every way, just as we are—yet was without sin." Hebrews 4:15, NIV. But if He did not take our fallen flesh or our human nature, His temptations were a sham. He could be tempted, yes; but not "just as we are." Such a "Christ" can claim all He likes, "Be of good cheer; I have overcome the world" (John 16:33), but His is a false boast, because the temptations of "the world [are] the lust of the flesh, and the lust of the eyes, and the pride of life" (1 John 2:16), and if Christ did not meet these temptations "in the flesh," He did not meet our temptations at all. "The enemy of Christ" is himself "a liar, and the father of lies" (John 8:44, NIV), and we can be sure he loves to make Christ out to be a liar by misrepresentation.

A popular Protestant view of Christ is on the same street as the immaculate conception, in fact, next door, as close as Sunday is to Sabbath. This is the idea that Christ took only the sinless nature of Adam before the Fall. In effect, this accomplishes the same objective, except that it transfers the unfair advantage for Christ from Mary's mother's womb to her own. Christ is effectively cut off from real connection with the fallen race. (Don't confuse this with the virgin birth, which the Bible teaches.) Even when Mary conceived Christ as a virgin, she could only pass on to Him *her* nature. But this extrabiblical idea again makes Christ out to be a kind of clever charlatan who tells us that He is "God with us" when He is millions of light-years away from us. For if He did not "come in the flesh" of humanity as it is, He did not come to be "with us" any more than a spaceman from another planet visiting us as a tourist.

Medieval Roman Catholic teaching saw Christ as "exempt" from the inheritance of our true human nature. The word *exempt* is a favorite word with Roman Catholics in discussing His nature: "The whole mind of the Oriental church ... drew from St. Augustine, the great Doctor of grace, those remarkable declarations which *exempt* the Blessed Virgin from all sin ...

"In the same spirit, and with a like implied *exemption* from the curse, St. Hippolytus, Bishop and Martyr, says, speaking first of our Saviour: 'He was the ark formed of corruptible wood. For by this is signified that His tabernacle was *exempt* from sin, of wood not obnoxious to corruption according to man; that is, of the Virgin, and of the Holy Ghost, covered within and without with the pure gold of the word of God.'"—Berington and Kirk, *The Faith of Catholics, Confirmed and Attested by the Fathers of the First Five Centuries of the Church,* vol. 3, pp. 443-446, emphasis supplied.

According to Scripture, Christ was "exempt" from nothing, for "the Lord hath laid on Him the iniquity of us all." Isaiah 53:6. His being "without sin" was not due to some prearranged "exemption" from meeting the full force of our human temptations.

What Christ Needs in Order to Be Our Substitute

When John says that Christ "has come in the flesh," he obviously does not mean some miraculous, or special kind that was unknown on this planet in his day. His good news is that this Christ has gained the victory of "authority" over our flesh and all its lusts, setting us free from its tyranny forever. He has worked no deceptive trick on us, pretending to be "God with us" while He cleverly avoided our identical battle with sin by taking a different kind of flesh or nature than we have.

Christ cannot be our Substitute unless He has met our temptations as we must meet them. He must meet our enemy on his own ground, in his own lair, and there slay him.

God's holy law demands from fallen man a righteousness that he cannot give because he has a problem in his "flesh." Paul says: "I am carnal [fleshly], sold under sin. ... The good that I would I do not: but the evil which I would not [do], that I do. Now if I do that I would not

[do], it is no more I that do it, but sin that dwelleth in me. ... Evil is present with me, ... warring against the law of my mind, and bringing me into captivity to the law of sin which is in my members. ... With the flesh [I serve] the law of sin." Romans 7:14-25.

Every man and woman on earth must confess that Paul knows what he is talking about. Sin has established a stranglehold on our nature. Its enticement and allurement are overwhelming. The Enemy of Christ has gloated that he has apparently invented a Frankenstein so strong that not a single human being, other than Christ, has ever escaped its tyranny. If he can prove that it is indeed impossible for human beings to vanquish sin in human flesh, he is well on his way to proving that God is wrong and he is right. And that would be only the last step before dethroning God. How could the universe ever respect a God whom Satan has proved wrong?

For this reason Satan has concocted a lie: Even Christ found sin so impossible to conquer in our flesh that He had to sidestep the encounter by the neat trick of taking the sinless nature of Adam before the fall. He maneuvers Christ into a position where He must virtually agree with His enemy that even He can't conquer our sin if He should take our nature, the nature of the sons and daughters of fallen Adam. In the process Christ is held up as deceptively claiming victory in a battle that never in fact took place.

How God Solved the Problem

After frankly detailing man's problem with "sin that dwelleth in me," Paul explains God's solution: "What the law could not do, in that it was weak through the flesh, God sending His own Son in the likeness of sinful flesh, and for sin, condemned sin in the flesh: that the righteousness of the law might be fulfilled in us, who walk not after the flesh, but after the Spirit." Romans 8:3, 4.

Christ has won the battle! Paul makes crystal clear what kind of flesh God has sent His son in—"the likeness of sinful flesh." The problem of entrenched sin is not in material things, but "in the flesh" of mankind. There is the lair where the beast, sin, has taken up his residence, where Christ must slay the dragon. This was no paper triumph, for He "condemned sin in the flesh," the flesh in which He came—our fallen nature.

Paul's word *likeness* cannot mean unlikeness, for it would be a monstrous fraud for Christ to profess to condemn sin in the flesh, the flesh in which Paul says we are "sold under sin" where "the law of sin" operates, if He counterfeited His incarnation by taking only what *appeared* to be our sinful flesh but which was not the real thing at all. It would leave Satan shouting "Foul!" to high heaven, which is what he does in the dogma of the immaculate conception. Paul uses the word *likeness* (with good reason) to denote the reality of Christ's full identity with us, yet making clear that He in no way participated in our sin. Christ's glorious victory lay in the fact that He was "tempted in every way, just as we are—yet was without sin." Hebrews 4:15, NIV. We have all *yielded* to temptations; He "*condemned* sin in the flesh" with all its allurements.

All the New Testament confirms this good news. "We were slaves to the elemental spirits of the universe. ... [But] God sent forth His Son, born of woman, born under the law, to redeem those who were under the law." Galatians 4:3-5, RSV. He entered the sphere where those spirits of sin were entrenched, and having invaded the enemy's territory, conquered.

"You, who were once estranged and hostile in mind [that's what sin is all about!], He has now reconciled in His body of flesh by His death." "He disarmed the principalities and powers and made a public example of them, triumphing over them." Colossians 1:21, 22; 2:15, RSV.

The letter to the Hebrews is emphatic. Christ "himself likewise took part of the same nature" as we, in order to meet the problem of our inner alienation, and to "deliver all those who through fear of death were subject to lifelong bondage." He "took" the heredity of Abraham, specifically not that of unfallen beings. "He had to be made like His brethren in every respect." Our salvation from sin is inextricably bound up with this truth: only in those areas where we are tempted is He "able to help those who are tempted." Hebrews 2:14-18, RSV. But since He has been tempted "just as we are," He stands revealed as a complete Saviour. James agrees with John and Paul. "Each person is tempted when he is lured and enticed by his own desire. Then desire when it has conceived gives birth to sin." James 1:14, 15, RSV. Temptation would be a sham for Christ and a deception if He did not feel the strength of that desire. But temptation from within is not sin; sensing the strength of the allurement is not a fall unless the temptation is yielded to. And that Christ never did. The glory of His righteousness is that it was the result of constant fierce conflict with temptation, "yet without sin." Thus His holiness is dynamic and glorious. He was "blameless, unstained, separated from sinners" (Hebrews 4:15, RSV) while He came close to redeem them where they are.

Thus the message of Christ's righteousness is tremendous. Have you ever stood by a lake in the evening while the moon is rising and seen that shimmering path of light stretch from your feet to the moon at the horizon's edge? Then as you walk down the shore, lo, the path of light moves with you, always stretching directly from where you are. I think of Christ's righteousness as something distinctly personal for "every man," a path devised by the Saviour to stretch from where my feet stand at this moment to His throne of grace and victory. He has put Himself in my place. He knows exactly the strength of the temptations now assailing me, and He knows how to resist. He was "made to be sin" for me. He knows the weight of the guilt I carry. He has tasted my despair, my disappointments. Nothing has escaped Him. He has even gone beyond everything I have experienced and has "tasted death," the second death, for me.

In fact, He is so fully and exactly my Substitute that He could come no closer if I were the only sinner in the world. He is my true other Self; I am "in Him" both legally and practically. No husband and wife are ever so close to each other as I am to Him through faith. Thus He "is able to save [me] to the uttermost," and He lives always for only one purpose: to "make intercession" for me, to plead in my behalf even against my own doubts against myself. See Hebrews 7:25.

Do you know how fierce battles with alluring temptation can be? Do you feel the powerful force of the riptide that would sweep you off your feet into the enticement of sin? Welcome to the human race! This is the problem Christ came to conquer. No wind of temptation ever beat upon us as fiercely as upon Christ, and no riptide ever swept us off our feet as strong as that which Christ braced Himself to withstand.

No matter who you are or where you are, you can know that One has stood exactly in your place, "yet without sinning." Look at Him, "see" Him, with all those clouds of deception blown away by the truth of His righteousness "in the likeness of sinful flesh." Believe that the sin that allures you has been "condemned in the flesh." You *can* overcome, through that faith in Him.

And not only 2000 years ago is He a Saviour. The good news is that He is working incessantly to make effective for us what He accomplished long ago. This work is not something taking place millions of light-years away. He is "a very present help in trouble." See Psalm 46:1.

We must now search for that link that binds justification by faith to the ministry of Christ in the heavenly sanctuary.

10

Christ's Sanctuary Ministry and Justification by Faith

For many, to hear of Christ's sanctuary ministry is almost like opening up a new world. Many readily believe that Christ ascended to heaven after His earthly life, but they have a nebulous idea of what He might be doing there. Is He on leave or vacation? Is He still resting up after His arduous task accomplished on earth? If He is working, what kind of work does He need to do? Didn't He finish His work of atonement when He died on the cross?

The word "High Priest" applied to Him describes His office and therefore the work He is doing now, but the term usually conjures up an ecclesiastical image remote from the everyday life where our problems are. What is the sanctuary where He is working? Is it a stained-glass retreat, dim and shadowy where mysterious ritual and religious mumbo jumbo go on in a heaven farther away than the Milky Way? Have the Father and the Son retired from involvement with human activity on this planet?

The Bible is so replete with references to Christ's high-priestly ministry in a heavenly sanctuary that endless books could be written about it. We can look only briefly.

Israel's ancient sanctuaries built by Moses, Solomon, Ezra and Nehemiah, and finally Herod were never the real thing. They were only a type of "the true tabernacle set up by the Lord" "in heaven." Hebrews 8:1, 2, NIV. All the blood of the countless animals offered in the earthly sanctuary could never suffice to wash away the stain of even one human sin. When David committed his monstrous sin of adultery and a cover-up murder, he knew well enough that no animal sacrifice could help him in the least. He prayed, "You do not delight in [such] sacrifice, or I would bring it. ... The sacrifices of God are a broken spirit; a broken and contrite heart." Psalm 51:16, NIV. The only effective sacrifice was always that offered by "the Lamb of God, who takes away the sin of the world." John 1:29, NIV. The earthly priests were only a "shadow" of Him as High Priest. The entire setup was a kindergarten lesson to illustrate Christ's work as Saviour. The "shadow" was as close as human consciousness could then come to envisaging the reality. See Hebrews 10:1.

The famous enemy of Christ (the antichrist), whose slimy trail weaves in and out through Christian history, has almost succeeded in eclipsing Christ's priestly ministry. Daniel foresaw this monstrous imposture in the vision he described in the eighth chapter of his book. His "little horn" is the same as John's "Enemy of Christ," the historical antichrist that "cast down the truth to the ground" and "prospered." Verse 12. This has been Satan's supreme achievement—corrupting the gospel message from within. For Daniel's benefit an angel inquired, "How long ... the vision, ... the transgression of desolation, to give both the [heavenly] sanctuary and the host to be trodden under foot?" Verse 13. The answer came in the famous 2300 day-year prophecy— "Then shall the sanctuary be cleansed [vindicated, justified, put right]." Verse 14. In other words, then shall the full truth of the gospel be set free to accomplish its God-intended work in preparing a people for the coming of Christ, a work to be done on earth which is parallel to and consistent with Christ's high-priestly ministry in heaven.

The heavenly sanctuary is the great nerve center, or if you please, military headquarters, where Christ directs His final battle against Satan to its ultimate victory. It is impossible to sense the meaning of life today except in the light of that sanctuary ministry. It is vital to a correct understanding of righteousness by faith. And, as we shall see, it is the only way to distinguish between the enemy's extremely clever counterfeit of the gospel and the truth concerning it. The sanctuary is the stage where the final great conflict of the ages will be decided and God's government vindicated.

Perhaps the most effective way of moving into this vital truth is by asking a few questions:

1. *Why is Jesus called our High Priest?* When we grasp what is involved, the term becomes an intimately endearing one. A high priest is all the following, comprised in one person:

(a) *Counselor.* The ancient high priest was looked up to as the wisest man in Israel. Your heavenly High Priest is your personal Counselor who will never give you wrong advice. "His name shall be called Wonderful, Counselor." Isaiah 9:6. "If any of you lack wisdom, he should ask God, who gives generously to all without finding fault." James 1:5, NIV.

(b) *Friend.* Christ is always "the friend ... of sinners." You will never again be lonely if you believe the gospel. Matthew 11:19; cf. John 15:15.

(c) *Physician.* He is the One "who healeth all thy diseases." Psalm 103:3.

(d) *Psychiatrist.* Everyone needs the services of this Psychiatrist who alone has power to restore in us our "right mind." Mark 5:15.

(e) *Business and finance manager.* "He shall direct thy paths." "So shall thy barns be filled with plenty." Proverbs 3:6, 10. "I will ... open you the windows of heaven, and pour you out a blessing, that there shall not be room enough to receive it." Malachi 3:10. If He cares about feeding the birds, won't He see that you have all the material advantages you need? See Matthew 6:26; Psalm 145:16.

(f) *Defense lawyer, advocate.* "If any man sin, we have an advocate with the Father, Jesus Christ the righteous." 1 John 2:1.

(g) *Intercessor, Friend at court.* "Because Jesus lives forever, he has a permanent priesthood. Therefore he is able to save completely those who come to God through him, because he always lives to intercede for them. Such a high priest meets our need." Hebrews 7:24-26, NIV. The Enemy of Christ is also our own personal enemy standing at our "right hand" to "resist" us. Zechariah gives a vivid picture of this court scene before the throne of God. But since "all things are naked and opened unto the eyes of Him with whom we have to do" (Hebrews 4:13), what Zechariah saw of Satan accusing us in "court" also reveals his present activities in trying to discourage us personally day by day. The "court" battle for our souls between Christ and Satan goes on both in the heavenly sanctuary and in our hearts here. See Zechariah 3:1-7. Christ is our Intercessor at the heavenly court; the Holy Spirit is our Intercessor in the same way here on earth right now. He intercedes between you and Satan, between you and etched neural patterns of the brain—providing the enabling grace to resist temptation and sinful habits. And the two scenes—heavenly and earthly—are interrelated, parallel, and consistent.

(h) *Elder Brother.* Those who have been fortunate to have a brother who has always been a friend can sense a little of what Christ is to us. There is a tie that binds one to such a brother even more intimately than to a father. Scripture speaks of our High Priest as being our Brother. See Hebrews 2:11; Matthew 28:10.

Please note that all this is what Christ is to us *today,* in genuine reality. All that is needed on our part to realize these priceless advantages is faith.

2. *How does the sanctuary truth illustrate the meaning of justification by faith in Christ?* One brief example will show the effectiveness of "faith in his blood."

When the sinner brought his innocent victim to be offered at the earthly sanctuary, he was required to take the knife and slay the animal himself. After leading the innocent victim all the way to the sanctuary, the sinner could not do this deed without a pang of remorse. The sight of the warm, flowing blood of the unresisting creature that had to die for his sin brought vividly to his mind the thought of Another who must die for him. Thoughtful Israelites always knew full well that "it is not possible that the blood of bulls and of goats should take away sins." Hebrews 10:4. "Without shedding of blood is no remission [of sin]." Hebrews 9:22. In other words, sin can never be "remitted"— that is, removed from our guilty hearts—except through the contrite realization that it was our hand that slew the divine Victim.

As surely as we all have by nature a "carnal mind [that] is enmity against God" (Romans 8:7), so surely has that enmity blossomed forth in the murderous deed of the ages, for "whosoever hateth his brother is a murderer" (1 John 3:15). The murder of the innocent Son of God was the full dimension of our sin. And through "faith in his blood" we have justification, including the healing of the enmity.

If the High Priest finished His work 2000 years ago, the entire sanctuary ministry is redundant, and Hebrews, with its emphasis on the heavenly sanctuary, has no right to a place in our New Testaments. If He has retired and the Holy Spirit alone is carrying on the work, the incarnation is rendered meaningless, for the ancient Levitical sanctuary service would in that case still suffice as a mere object lesson of what the Lamb of God did *for* us when He was "slain from the foundation of the world." Revelation 13:8.

But it is specifically as a High Priest in the heavenly sanctuary that Christ does His work of saving "them to the uttermost that come unto God by Him." And justification by faith is the actual saving! It is the subject matter of His ever living "to make intercession for them." Hebrews 7:25. Hebrews therefore discloses the intimate relationship of justification by faith in its fullest sense to the sanctuary ministry.

3. *What is the "atonement" provided through the sanctuary ministry?* Atonement is simply reconciliation, being at-one-with God. It is not that God is reconciled to us, for He already so loved the world that He gave His Son to die for us.

"Be *ye* reconciled to God" is the message of the gospel. 2 Corinthians 5:20. The sacrifice of the cross providing the basis for man's salvation was complete and final, but not yet can it be truly said that the practical effects of reconciliation are complete. Since the atonement is reconciliation with God, it is obvious that those who still have "the carnal mind" are not yet reconciled to Him, for such a mind is still in a state of "enmity against God." If Paul, writing years after the cross, could say to the Corinthians, "Ye are yet carnal" (1 Corinthians 3:3), he meant that they had not yet truly "received the atonement" (Romans 5:11).

The legal or forensic justification provided at the cross is based on God's offering and gift for "all men"; but not until the sinner hears the good news and believes does he experience justification *by faith*. So the atonement must be not only provided legally by God, but received by the sinner through faith.

This makes clear the need for a final atonement in the sense of a culminating growth of faith which heals all latent or buried enmity against God in the heart and mind of the believer. This is the work that the enemy of Christ, the antichrist, has determined to oppose to the bitter end, for if he can succeed in nullifying the final atonement, by retrospect he can nullify the atonement provided at the cross, and thus even yet win the final battle of the conflict of the ages.

This invests with solemn significance the message of the cleansing of the heavenly sanctuary. The Scripture doctrine of atonement itself is vitally involved and it is nullified if there is no cosmic Day of Atonement as prophesied in Daniel 8 and 9 and taught in type by the sanctuary service.

Are Adventists not commanded to be foremost in uplifting Christ before the world? But such a witness is not to be merely a "me too" echo of an evangelical chorus that sets forth a very limited view of justification by faith. The final great battle between Christ and Satan is a death grapple with the fundamental realities of how God deals with sin itself, and a special witness is imperative. To destroy the cleansing of the heavenly sanctuary is to destroy Calvary, for the former is the logical necessity and unveiling of the latter.

This basic relationship between Christ's work on the cross and His work in the heavenly sanctuary is well summed up in the following quotation: "The intercession of Christ in man's behalf in the sanctuary above is as essential to the plan of salvation as was His death upon the cross. By His death He began that work which after His resurrection He ascended to complete in heaven."—Ellen G. White, *The Great Controversy,* p. 489.

The almost universal acceptance of the pagan-papal teaching of natural immortality has all but eclipsed selfless New Testament *agape,* so that the cross for millions is robbed of its true glory and power.* Modern history has demonstrated that it is only through the conception of the second-apartment ministry of the High Priest that this New Testament concept of love revealed in the cross is restored. The work of unveiling "the breadth, and length, and depth, and height" of "the *agape* of Christ" as the infinite giving of Himself to the equivalent of "the second death" is associated with the heavenly High Priest's work of final atonement. The magnificent results are to be seen in a people who sense the constraint of that love to the fullest, demonstrating that indeed *agape* is the fulfilling of the law. This is to be a beautiful and welcome sight to the heavenly universe, and the actual finishing of the gospel commission.

Ellen White seems to offer the profound insight that the concept of *agape* is best understood when Christ is clearly perceived as our High Priest in the Most Holy Apartment of the heavenly sanctuary. See *Early Writings,* pp. 55, 56.

---

* Lutheran, Anders Nygren, recognizes that wherever there is "belief in the soul's natural immortality" "the egocentric will is in evidence." Thus, "this idea of the natural immortality of the soul is completely foreign to the *Agape* motif." *Agape and Eros* (London: S.P.C.K., 1957), pp. 164, 180, 224.

4. *Why the final Day of Atonement?* In the ancient "shadow" service of the earthly sanctuary, the Day of Atonement closed the annual cycle of reconciliation ministry. It symbolized the ultimate conquest of sin and its effects as well as the destruction of its impenitent originator and perpetrators.

Since the lair of sin is the "flesh" or sinful nature of fallen man, it is impossible that the real Day of Atonement can bring the reign of sin to an end until the problem of continued sinning in those who believe the gospel is solved. A purely and exclusively legal declaration of justification without a justification by faith that reconciles the believer's heart to God's righteousness would defeat the entire sanctuary ministry.

It's as if a cosmic chess game were being played out in the realm of salvation. Satan would like to make a move that will checkmate Christ, and this he can accomplish if he can ensure that sinning is perpetuated. Paul makes this clear: "What the law could not do, in that it was weak through the flesh, God sending His own Son in the likeness of sinful flesh, and for sin, condemned sin in the flesh: that the righteousness of the law might be fulfilled in us, who walk not after the flesh, but after the Spirit." Romans 8:3, 4.

Satan may be willing through force of circumstances to concede that Christ in His incarnation "condemned sin in the flesh," but his checkmate strategy is to block "the righteousness of the law" from being "fulfilled in us." His device for accomplishing this is a counterfeit version of justification by faith.

The heavenly Day of Atonement and Daniel's cleansing of the sanctuary (Daniel 8:14) are one and the same thing. As the sins of the ancient Israelites were symbolically or typically transferred to the sanctuary, so in reality all the sins of those who profess faith in Christ are loaded on the government of God. He assumes the guilt of them all. Satan challenges Christ to dispose of the problem. No legal fiction can ever conclude the great conflict of the ages. Unless Christ's people cooperate with Him in the final disposition of sin, the heavenly sanctuary can never be cleansed, or vindicated, or put right.

Part of the Enemy's clever strategy seems to be to label all concern for overcoming sin as the heresy of "perfectionism," a subtle attempt to preserve the status quo of Satan's supposed triumph. He boasts that he has invented a device that is more than a match for God: sin, which in fallen human nature he claims is unconquerable. Hence the attempt to prove (a) that Christ could not have conquered Satan's invention of sin if He had taken on Himself our fallen nature, and (b) that it is impossible for any believer in Christ to overcome sin itself so long as he still possesses his fallen nature. The best he can do is to try to be "less sinful," while the principle of sin is left intact. These are two sides of one coin, both in conflict with the Bible concept of the cleansing of the sanctuary.

In spite of numerous "scholarly" denials, Scripture is clear that the Old Testament Day of Atonement ministry vitally concerned the Israelite believers, for "on that day ye may be clean from all your sins before the Lord." Leviticus 16:30. The antitypical Day of Atonement likewise involves God's people especially since 1844. God's promise is that He will have a people of whom He can say in all honesty, "Here are they that keep the commandments of God, and the faith of Jesus." Revelation 14:12. The full context indicates that this will be the practical fruitage of the cleansing of the heavenly sanctuary.

5. *How is justification by faith related to the vindication of Christ in the cleansing of the heavenly sanctuary?* God's people grow "from faith to faith" and thus reveal and make possible the full scope of the gospel unto salvation. Romans 1:16, 17. Always Christ's righteousness, His doing and dying, remains the only basis of their justification (that is, their righteousness); never do they acquire even a trace element of merit in themselves. But their *appreciation* of the sacrificial love involved in His doing and dying grows to the point where they become mature in Christ. And since they cooperate with their High Priest in His cleansing of the sanctuary, they do so through a complete reception of His righteousness. They are truly justified by faith.

It's like a woman who loves a man. She becomes mature in understanding and appreciating him so as to stand by his side in marriage. The denouement of the great drama of the ages is the marriage of the Lamb. This is the great plot of the Bible itself, which reaches its climax in Revelation 19. The Father, Christ, and all the holy angels have been "ready" for a long time; at last it can be said that "His wife hath made herself ready." Revelation 19:7. Then can come the vindication of Christ, because any reticence on the part of His bride to commit herself to Him in the complete surrender implied in marriage involves not only immaturity, but at least a partial rejection of Him. And this is to His shame as a Bridegroom.

In other words, the childish motive prevents "the marriage of the Lamb" from taking place. Such an idea in respect of Christ becomes a tool of the enemy's strategy.

If the great unnumbered hosts assembled at the final assize of the ages must watch Christ's bride-to-be push Him from her while she reaches for the cake and ice cream that come with the wedding, they would be horrified. Not that it is wrong for the little flower girl to reach for the cake and ice cream; but the tragedy of the ages would be for the bride of Christ to be so immature that she is insensitive to His maturity of love and has no mature appreciation for His sacrifice. This would become at last the ultimate unbelief or nonfaith and, of course, a contradiction of justification by faith.

In her poem "The Ninety and Nine," it is one thing for Elizabeth Clephane to say,

> "But none of the ransomed ever knew
>   How deep were the waters crossed,
> Nor how dark was the night that the Lord passed through
>   Ere He found His sheep that was lost."

But it is another thing for His bride, His ransomed one who must meet Him at the wedding, to be content not to appreciate "how deep" those waters were. The pathetic spectacle that greets heaven and earth today is the sight of a "bride" who has very little appreciation for the depth of her Bridegroom's character of love. She is engrossed with the materialistic and sensual pleasures of the world that she offers her Bridegroom the barest minimum of devotion. Her heart is absorbed in this world's cares and amusements, not on pleasing her Lover. Such non-faith is entirely inconsistent with justification by faith.

6. *How does the truth of the sanctuary enable us to distinguish between Satan's counterfeit justification by faith and the genuine thing?* Several Scripture facts may help make this clear:

(a) The Enemy's supreme weapon in his warfare against Christ is the business of counterfeiting. He is known as the one "which deceiveth the whole world." "He is a liar, and the father of it." Revelation 12:9; John 8:44.

(b) His masterpiece of deception is the assumption of the role of a counterfeit Christ. "This is that spirit of antichrist, … already … in the world." 1 John 4:3. "Satan himself is transformed into an angel of light" (2 Corinthians 11:14)—a "false Christ" (Matthew 24:24).

(c) The prophecies of Daniel and Revelation describe the last-day success of Satan under the symbols of "the little horn" and the "beast," a power which professes to worship Christ and even purports to bring revival and reformation to the world. Daniel 7, 8; Revelation 13:1-17. This includes of course a counterfeit justification by faith.

(d) The word *antichrist* means one who pretends to stand in the place of Christ while actually underhandedly opposing Him. Being a finite angel, learning to perfect his deceptive skills as time goes on, Satan assumes his most effective role as a counterfeit high priest. His spirit becomes, of necessity, a counterfeit "holy spirit," and he perfects a technique of working miracles to establish his claims to the worship of sincere but badly deceived Christian people. Revelation 13:13, 14. He is largely the source of the wonderworking spiritual phenomena in the last days, including miracles of healing. See Revelation 16:14; 2 Corinthians 11:15.

(e) The division of the sanctuary into two apartments with a daily and annual ministry of the high priest is a symbol of a significant division in Christ's heavenly high-priestly service. Hebrews 9:1-12.* Daniel was obviously familiar with the Levitical service and would naturally understand the cleansing or vindication of the sanctuary at the end of 2300 days-years to mean the heavenly Day of Atonement. Daniel was intelligent and well-informed. His vision was far wider than the narrow confines of Judaism. It was by no means beyond his capacity to envisage a cosmic Day of Atonement which would eventually conclude sinful world history. This would require on the part of Christ another phase of high-priestly ministry corresponding to that of the Levitical Day of Atonement. Since the Saviour's grand work is that of justification or righteousness by faith, the implications of His sanctuary ministry for a true understanding of righteousness by faith are stupendous.

---

* Hebrews is not concerned with detailing the two-apartment heavenly ministry, but clearly states that the two-apartment aspect of the sanctuary is "a shadow of good things to come." Hebrews 10:1. Thus it supports implicitly the idea of a significant division in the heavenly ministry of Christ as High Priest.

As Daniel and Revelation are complementary in their prophetic scope, we find that John witnessed the inauguration of the great Day of Atonement in the events he describes as the sounding of the "seventh trumpet." Here he was shown the opening of the most holy apartment, whereas in previous visions he had seen the first, the holy apartment, opened. See Revelation 11:15-19; cf. Revelation 1:12, 20; 8:3-5. This would clearly imply the closing of the ministry previously centered in the first apartment. Christ's message "to the angel of the church in Philadelphia" symbolizes a period near the end of time; there we see the work of the heavenly High Priest who "openeth, and no man shutteth; and shutteth, and no man openeth. ... I have set before thee an open door, and no man can shut it." Revelation 3:7, 8. This message is meaningless unless it refers to the beginning of the Day of Atonement. In opening the door of the most holy apartment, Christ automatically shuts the door of the first. On the ancient Day of Atonement no priest functioned in the first apartment while the high priest was in the second.

In speaking of this sanctuary ministry, we employ the same terms as found in Scripture. It is pointless to question just how literal is the idea of a first and second apartment in terms of spatial design. If God in His wisdom saw best to represent these vast spiritual truths in this kind of verbal coinage, we would be wise to accept them and let the Holy Spirit impart the larger dimensions of spiritual perception they are designed to convey.

(f) The antichrist's last opportunity to "deceive the whole world" would be to divert the attention of God's people away from our Lord's change of ministry in the Heavenly Sanctuary. He wants to nullify the distinctiveness of Christ's last-phase work. Satan's purpose in so doing is to separate God's people from continuing and growing fellowship with their High Priest in His closing work and to prevent the second coming of Christ. "Satan invents unnumbered schemes to occupy our minds, that they may not dwell upon the very work with which we ought to be best acquainted. The archdeceiver hates the great truths that bring to view an atoning sacrifice and an all-powerful mediator. He knows that with him everything depends on his diverting minds from Jesus and His truth. ... All need a knowledge for themselves of the position and work of their great High Priest."—Ellen G. White, *The Great Controversy*, p. 488.

This heavenly change from one phase to another of Christ's ministry gives Satan the opportunity he once had with the ancient Jews. After Christ as true High Priest had ascended to heaven to minister in the sanctuary there, the Jews continued to center their attention on the now-defunct rituals in the earthly temple which Jesus said "is left unto you desolate." Matthew 23:38. They were deceived to their ruin.

Likewise today, any attempt to restrict Christ's work to that symbolized by the first-apartment ministry exposes the worshiper to the same terrible danger of clever deception by the antichrist. He has perfected his techniques now to the point of bestowing "power" on his adherents, and a kind of "light" that is pleasing to sophistry-loving minds. But this is not the true power of the genuine Holy Spirit of God. See *Early Writings*, p. 56.

A clear example of the truth versus counterfeit options is the existence of two separate and distinct streams of justification-by-faith teaching in the world today. One is centered in an appreciation of God's true character of *agape*, which sees the cross of Christ as a perfect blend of God's justice and mercy so that He can be just and the justifier of those who have faith in Christ. Such faith works by love and invariably leads to obedience to all the commandments of God, including the widely disregarded fourth, which teaches the observance of the true Lord's day, the seventh-day Sabbath. This stream of justification by faith, emphasizing the twin gifts of both pardon and power, upholds the law of God while it also reveals His incomparable love. It is salvation from sin, not in it. The faith that operates in this justification by faith accomplishes in believing human hearts a work of complete atonement and prepares a people for the coming of Christ as symbolized by the bride making herself ready for the marriage.

The other stream of justification by faith is centered in a deficient view of the love of God, which sees His character in a distorted light far short of the dimensions of *agape*. The teaching of natural immortality distorts the picture so that the love of God merely lends His Son to humanity rather than giving Him. No clear concept of "the second death" which Christ suffered on the cross is possible. In turn, faith is devalued to become an egocentric "trust" based on human insecurity and a search for false "assurance" of salvation in sin rather than from it. The teaching of righteousness by faith is thus severely limited in that the pardon of justification is unduly emphasized at the expense of the power of the Spirit available in sanctification. True *agape* being absent, faith in this view does not work to produce obedience to all of God's commandments; a counterfeit sabbath is also widely accepted as a substitute for the true Lord's day, along with other unbiblical doctrines. The law of God is denigrated either by the teaching that it has been virtually abolished, or that it is impossible for anyone to obey truly. Totally lacking in this stream is any concept of the cleansing of the heavenly sanctuary or the preparation of a people for the coming of Christ.

The ministry of Christ in the most holy apartment will accomplish in those who follow Him by faith the restoration of the image of God in character, a character *of agape.* The revelation of this love becomes the final proclamation of the everlasting gospel to the world. But the work of the Enemy of Christ in his counterfeit role as antichrist provides the superficial criteria of conversion without the true insignia of *agape.* Therefore the ministries of both Christ and the antichrist proceed simultaneously to where all the world lines up on one side or the other. Christ reaps "the harvest of the earth" in the development of a people who resemble Him in character; the antichrist presents "the clusters of the vine of the earth; for her grapes [of wrath] are fully ripe." Revelation 14:15, 20.

7. *If the Lord forgives our sins when we confess them, why is a "blotting out of sins" necessary on the Day of Atonement?* In a legal or forensic sense our sins were forgiven when Christ died on His cross long ago, for "God was in Christ, ... not imputing their [the world's] trespasses unto them." 2 Corinthians 5:19. He is completely sincere in forgiving our sins and giving us the assurance of forgiveness when we repent and confess. The reason why the blotting out of sins is necessary in the Day of Atonement is not because of any halfhearted forgiveness on God's part, but because we sinful mortals are notoriously halfhearted in our repentance.

Will anyone ever read this book who has never backslidden? We all have. The Bible is replete with examples of people who have repented and were converted, but who later fell dismally. David, converted king and prophet, author of many of our beloved psalms, committed adultery with Bathsheba and then murder; Peter, baptized, ordained apostle, was sure he would never deny Christ, but before sunrise he failed miserably three times; Hezekiah, pious king of Judah, walked before the Lord with what he thought was "a perfect heart," yet sinned grievously after his miraculous healing; even Moses, with whom the Lord talked face-to-face, lost his temper on the borders of the Promised Land.

These people had all lived in a saving relationship—until they withdrew from that relationship. They fell because of unrealized and therefore unconfessed sin which all the while lay deep and unseen in their hearts. When we are aware of a sin and confess it, we are indeed forgiven; but John's promise in 1 John 1:9 does not mean that such forgiveness is a blanket to cover all buried sins yet to be confessed. If we remain committed, the Holy Spirit will continue to convict us of sin hitherto unknown but deep within.

As we respond positively, our confession of sin becomes ever deeper, until in His infinite wisdom God sees that the last root of alienation has been torn from the heart. This is equivalent to receiving the seal of God, or the blotting out of sin. It means that the penitent has learned to hate sin "even as" Christ hated it, and thus he has "overcome even as" Christ also "overcame."

Then the decree goes forth, "He that is holy, let him be holy still." Revelation 22:11.

Under Law or Under Grace?

If our understanding of our inheritance in Christ has grown so that we can appreciate Him as our High Priest, we can make an intelligent choice as to where we will stand. Our privilege is as follows: "Sin shall not have dominion over you: for ye are not under the law, but under grace." Romans 6:14.

To be under the law means to be a slave concerned for one's own security, out of our fear of being lost in the darkness and emptiness of hell. This is still a form of selfishness, although a highly refined one, to be sure. One can't blame the misinformed Yale professor who mocks Christianity by saying it is only "just another form of giving up the present for some goal."—Charles Reich, *The Greening of America* (New York: Random House, 1970), p. 301. All egocentric motivation is what Paul meant by his phrase, "under the law." It is being under the constraint imposed by a fear of the punishment that the law can inflict, for "the law worketh wrath." Romans 4:15. Many Evangelicals frankly admit that the only motivation they know that can work is that of fear of this "wrath." An example is an African Evangelical theologian who says that "only the presupposition of eternal torment in fire … will keep the fervor of evangelism burning."—Byang H. Cato, *Theological Pitfalls in Africa,* (Kismu, Kenya: Evangel Publishing House, 1975), p. 149. This is an admission of gospel bankruptcy.

But to be under grace is to sense the constraint of a new motivation, a sense of soul-consuming gratitude for redemption, an awesome appreciation of a love that has infinite dimensions of length, breadth, depth, and height, measured by the arms of Christ's cross.

Obedience, loyalty, purity, devotion—these are not goals we work toward; they are gifts we discover in our response to His open arms of love and forgiveness. "Sin *shall not* have dominion over you." In this new captivity to grace we discover freedom at last.

We want to nudge Paul to move over so we can kneel down beside him: "God forbid that I should boast of anything but the cross of our Lord Jesus Christ, through which the world is crucified to me and I to the world." Galatians 6:14, NEB. "For me to live is Christ." Philippians 1:21.

This is the beginning of everlasting life, a new quality of life. You have passed from death unto life. You are a citizen of heaven, a new kind of person in Christ, for you have believed the gospel to be what it is—good news.